Nick Vandome

Dreamweaver CS3

in
easy steps

In easy steps is an imprint of Computer Step
Southfield Road · Southam
Warwickshire CV47 0FB · United Kingdom
www.ineasysteps.com

Notice of Liability
Every effort has been made to ensure that this book contains accurate and current information. However, Computer Step and the author shall not be liable for any loss or damage suffered by readers as a result of any information contained herein.

Trademarks
Dreamweaver® is a registered trademark of Adobe Systems Incorporated. All other trademarks are acknowledged as belonging to their respective companies.

Printed and bound in the United Kingdom

ISBN-13 978-1-84078-348-3
ISBN-10 1-84078-348-6

Contents

4 Working with images 63

5 Using CSS 75

6 Formatting with CSS 91

11 Advanced features 159

12 Publishing 175

Index 187

1 About Dreamweaver

Dreamweaver is a powerful web authoring tool that can be used to create highly professional websites. This chapter looks at the user interface of the program and explains some of the features that will enable you to start working at creating web pages. These include the Insert panel, the Properties Inspector and the Dreamweaver toolbars. It also shows how to use external editors for content.

Introducing Dreamweaver

In the early days of web design, the code used to create web pages was entered manually. This required the page designers to have a reasonable knowledge of the language, Hypertext Markup Language (HTML), in which it is written. While this is not a full-blown computer language and it can be learned reasonably quickly, it can be a time-consuming business to create websites in this fashion.

The next development in web-design software was the introduction of HTML editors. These are programs that help make the process of creating HTML code quicker and easier by giving the author shortcuts for adding the elements that make up the coded page. However, this still requires a good basic knowledge of HTML: it makes the process quicker for the experienced designer but it does not help the novice much.

The big breakthrough in web-design software, and one that introduced a huge new audience to the joys of web design, was the introduction of WYSIWYG programs. WYSIWYG stands for "what you see is what you get", and they enable people to design their own web pages without even having to be aware of the existence of HTML. They work in a similar way to a word-processing or a desktop-publishing program: what you lay out on the screen is what the end user will see on their computer. With these programs, the HTML is still present (and you can edit it manually if you desire) but it is all generated automatically by the program in the background.

Dreamweaver is primarily a WYSIWYG web authoring program that provides an effective interface for quickly creating high-quality web pages. In addition, it contains a range of powerful tools for incorporating the latest web-design elements into sites to give them a highly professional look. Overall, Dreamweaver is an ideal program for anyone involved in designing websites: its combination of simplicity and power makes it an excellent choice for the novice and the professional alike. For the experienced web designer, Dreamweaver CS3 also has improved functions for using cascading style sheets and for creating dynamic web pages – these are used in conjunction with databases and can change depending on the user's requirements.

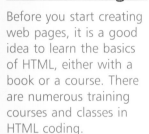

Don't forget

Before you start creating web pages, it is a good idea to learn the basics of HTML, either with a book or a course. There are numerous training courses and classes in HTML coding.

Don't forget

Even when you are using a WYSIWYG web authoring program, it is still important to follow the basics of good web design.

Don't forget

In 2005 Adobe completed the acquisition of Macromedia, the creators of Dreamweaver.

Start screen

In order to help rationalize the number of options that are available when Dreamweaver is first opened, the latest version has a Start screen that appears initially, or when no other documents are open. The Start screen contains a variety of options for opening and creating documents and also obtaining help on using Dreamweaver CS3:

Click here to open a previously viewed file

Click here to create a new file

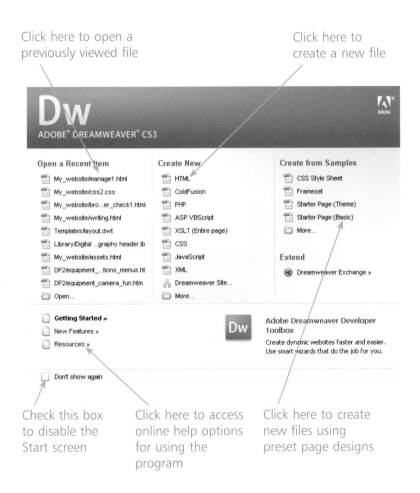

Hot tip

Click on the Dreamweaver Exchange link to access the Adobe website for items that can be used to expand the functionality of Dreamweaver.

Check this box to disable the Start screen

Click here to access online help options for using the program

Click here to create new files using preset page designs

Workspaces

Designer workspace (Windows and Mac)

This is the default workspace and it enables you to create WYSIWYG web pages by placing graphical and textual elements in the workspace, knowing that this is how they should appear in a browser. The Designer workspace also has options for entering HTML code by hand and even viewing the code and the graphical interface simultaneously. The main elements of the Designer workspace are:

Insert toolbar (often-used elements)   Code view   Code and Design view   Design view

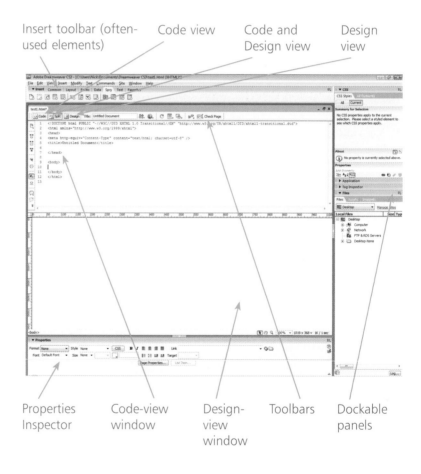

Properties Inspector   Code-view window   Design-view window   Toolbars   Dockable panels

Coder workspace (Windows only)

This is the workspace for people who want to work primarily with handwritten HTML code. It is a powerful HTML editor, so hand-coders can now enjoy the same power and versatility as those working with the graphical interface. In the Coder workspace, the same elements can be inserted as with the Designer workspace, but the default is Code view. The main elements of the Coder workspace are:

Dockable panels

Insert toolbar (often-used elements)

View (Code, Code and Design and Design) icons – see previous page

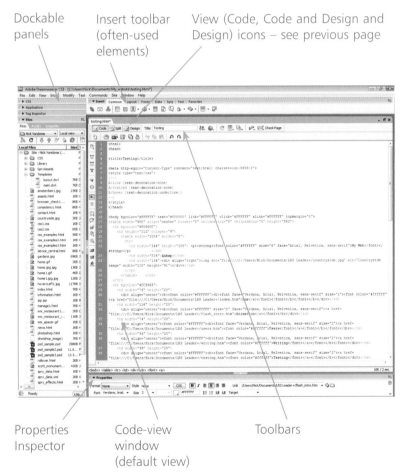

Properties Inspector

Code-view window (default view)

Toolbars

Don't forget

The different workspaces can be accessed by selecting Window, Workspace Layout from the menu bar. The Mac version does not have the Coder option.

11

Preferences

Dreamweaver offers extensive options for the way the program looks and operates. These are located via the Preferences window. The preferences can be used to change the way the program and its elements appear, and also to change the way certain tasks are performed. There are 20 categories of preferences and each category has several options. The Preferences options can be accessed by selecting Edit, Preferences (Windows) or Dreamweaver, Preferences (Mac) from the menu bar. Once the Preferences window has been accessed it can be used to customize numerous elements of the program:

 Click here to select a category of preferences

12

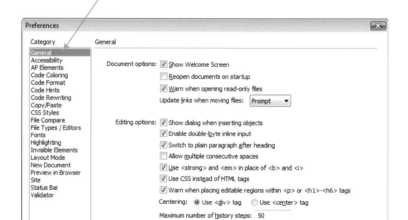

 Select category options here and click OK to apply them

Working with panels

Panels in Dreamweaver CS3 contain numerous options for creating and editing content. They are docked along the side and top of the working environment to allow more space when designing pages. The panels can be selected from the Window menu on the menu bar. Once panels have been accessed, there are various ways in which to work with them.

1 Click and drag here to move a panel set

2 Click here to access a panel menu

Don't forget

Panels are grouped in logical combinations that perform similar general tasks within Dreamweaver.

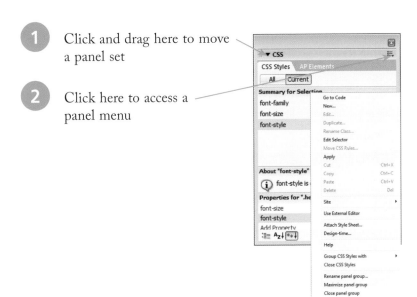

3 Click here to expand or collapse a panel

Hot tip

To move a panel from its current set, select Group [panel name] With from the panel menu. You can then select another panel set with which to group the selected panel, or select New Panel Group from the menu to create it in a set of its own.

13

4 To close a panel, click here (Mac) or here (Windows)

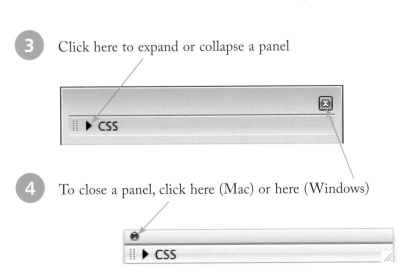

Insert panel

The Insert panel is the one that is used most frequently for adding content to web pages. It can be viewed in a tabbed or a menu format:

Menu format. Click here to access the Insert-panel options

Click here to access an item within the selected category

Tabbed format. Click here to access the Insert-panel options

Click here to access an item within the selected category

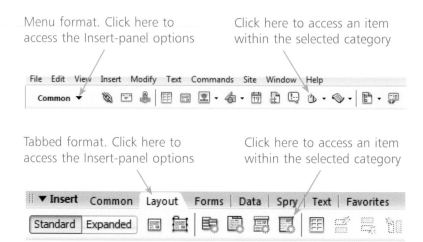

The Insert panel can be accessed by selecting Window, Insert from the menu bar, or View, Toolbars, Insert from the menu bar.

Moving between formats

To move between the Menu and Tabbed formats of the Insert panel:

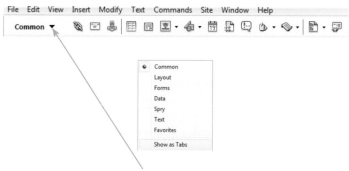

In Menu format, click here and select Show as Tabs

In Tabbed format, click here and select Show as Menu

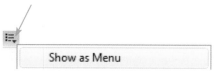

Common

This is the default setting and the one that contains some of the most commonly used elements on a web page, such as hyperlinks, tables, images and templates.

Layout

This provides options for creating tables, layers and frames. It also provides various options for viewing tables.

Forms

This contains all of the elements that are used in online forms. For more information about this, see Chapter 11.

Data

This contains buttons that can be used to insert data into the head section of a web page. This can include items such as metadata, keywords and descriptions. It also has options for adding scripts, such as Javascript, into an HTML document.

Spry

This contains buttons that can be used to insert Spry elements into a web page. These are a collection of items that can be added to web pages to create an improved experience for users. Spry elements are created with a combination of Javascript, cascading style sheets and HTML, and include items such as expanding menu bars and text-validation areas. For more information on working with Spry elements see Chapter 9.

Text

This contains buttons for inserting text functions, including bold, italics, preformatted text, headings and lists. Some of these functions are also available on the Text Property Inspector and also from the Text menu on the menu bar.

Favorites

This can be used to create a custom list of the most frequently used items within the Insert panel. To add Favorites, right-click (Ctrl+click on the Mac) on the Insert panel and select the required items in the Customize Favorites Objects window.

Don't forget

The head part of an HTML document contains information that is not displayed on the published page. One function of head information is to help search engines locate a page on the web.

15

Properties Inspector

The Properties Inspector displays the attributes of the currently selected item on the page, whether it is an image, a piece of text, a table, a frame or an element of multimedia. In addition to viewing these attributes, you can alter them by entering values within the Properties Inspector. For instance, if you want to change the size of an image, you can select it and then enter the new size that is required. To display the properties of a particular element it has to be selected first.

Image properties

Select an image by clicking on it once to display the relevant Properties Inspector:

Size   Dimensions   Location   Alt tag

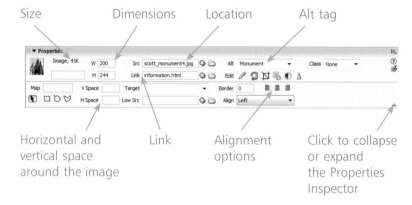

Horizontal and vertical space around the image   Link   Alignment options   Click to collapse or expand the Properties Inspector

Text properties

Select a paragraph of text by inserting the cursor anywhere within it, or select specific pieces of text by clicking and dragging the cursor over them:

Format   Font   Style   Color   Bold and italic

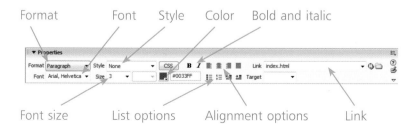

Font size   List options   Alignment options   Link

External editors

When designing web pages, you will be working with a lot of elements that cannot be edited directly within Dreamweaver. These can include elements such as sound files or movie clips, and also images (although some editing can be done on images directly within Dreamweaver). One way to edit them would be to do so in an appropriate program before they are inserted into Dreamweaver. However, if you then need to edit the items again, once they have been imported, it can be frustrating having to open up the file again, edit it, and then re-import it. Dreamweaver simplifies this process by providing direct links to external editors that can be used to edit items while they are still in the Dreamweaver environment.

It is possible to specify which program you want to use for specific tasks, e.g. editing images, by selecting the file type and the program from the File Types / Editors category of the Preferences window:

1 Select Edit, Preferences from the menu bar and select the File Types / Editors category

2 Click here to select a file type

3 Click here to select an external editor from your hard drive

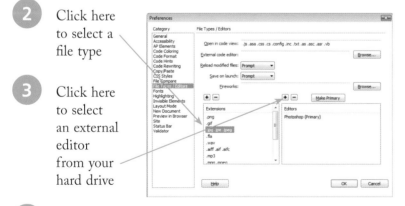

4 Click OK

...cont'd

Using external editors

Once you have selected the required external editors for different file formats, it is then possible to access them while you are working on a page:

 Select an element on a page, such as an image

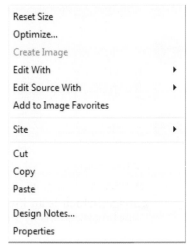 Right-click (Windows) or Ctrl+click (Mac) on the item and select the Edit With option that contains the primary editor for the selected item. To edit the item with a different editor, select Edit With and then browse to the program that you want to use to edit the selected item

To change the external editor for a specific file type at any time, select Edit, Edit with External Editor from the menu bar and change the selection in the File Types / Editors dialog box, as shown on the last page

Page properties

In addition to setting preferences that affect all of the files you work on in Dreamweaver, it is possible to set properties for individual pages. These include items such as background color, the color of links and the margins on the page. To set page properties:

1 Select Modify, Page Properties from the menu bar

2 Click here to select attributes for options such as background images, text color, background color and default page font

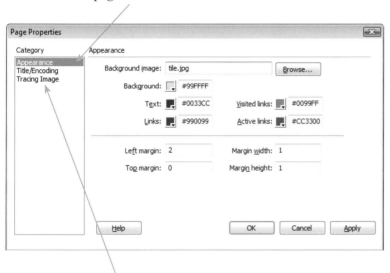

3 Click here to select other categories for the page properties. These include document title and tracing image (which is an image comprising a page design that can be inserted into a file and used as the basis to create the actual page)

19

Don't forget

Hyperlinks, or just links, can be colored differently depending on their current state. Different colors can be applied for a link before it has been activated, after it has been activated and when it is in the state of being pressed.

Beware

If you are using a background image on a web page, make sure it is not too complex or gaudy. This could create a dramatic initial effect, but if people are looking at the page a lot it could become irritating. Similarly, background colors should, in general, be subtle and unobtrusive, rather than bright and bold. White is a very effective background for pages.

Page tabs

Almost invariably when a website is being created, a lot of different pages will be open at the same time. Keeping track of all of the open pages can be confusing, particularly if you are switching between different pages regularly. Dreamweaver CS3 has simplified this problem by displaying all of the open pages in the form of tabs at the top of each page. This means that, provided your monitor is large enough, all of the open documents can be viewed and accessed at any time.

Click on a tab to move to that open document. This can be done with any open document

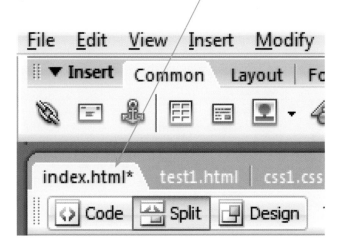

Hot tip

If an open file has an asterisk next to its name, this means that changes have been made and not yet saved. When the file is saved the asterisk disappears.

For Dreamweaver on the Mac, pages are tabbed in the same way as for the Windows version, and files can also be closed by clicking on this icon for each individual file

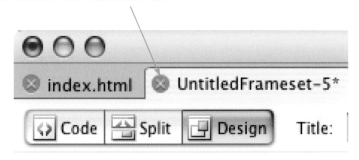

Toolbars

Dreamweaver CS3 has a number of toolbars that contain several options for specifying how the program operates. By default these are displayed at the top of the page, although they can also be dragged to other locations. The toolbars can be accessed by selecting View, Toolbars from the menu bar. (The Insert panel is also available from the Toolbars menu, as it is from the Window option on the menu bar.) The two most commonly used toolbars are the Document one and the Standard one. The features of these include:

Document toolbar

Page views · Page title · Get or put files · Refresh · Visual aids

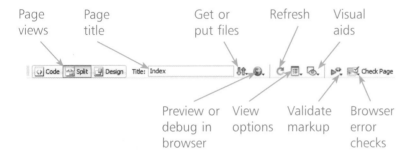

Preview or debug in browser · View options · Validate markup · Browser error checks

Standard toolbar

New · Browse in Bridge · Save · Print code · Copy

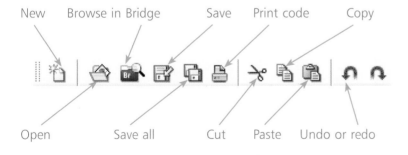

Open · Save all · Cut · Paste · Undo or redo

Don't forget

The page-views options on the toolbar allow you to switch between the graphical layout and the HTML layout, or use a combination of the two.

Don't forget

Browse in Bridge takes you to Adobe Bridge, which is a stand-alone program for browsing files and looking for shared assets, particularly images, in other programs.

Don't forget

The other available toolbars are Insert (the Insert panel), Style Rendering for creating pages for different output devices, and Coding for working with code in Code view.

Creating pages

When creating new pages after File, New is selected from the menu bar, Dreamweaver CS3 offers considerable flexibility. You may if you wish create a blank page (with no formatting or pre-inserted elements) by selecting Blank Page, HTML, but there are a lot more options available to you:

1 Select File, New from the menu bar

2 Click on the Blank Page tab

Don't forget

By default, basic HTML pages are created as XHTML files. This is a version of HTML that enables documents to be used in an XML environment, if required. The default document type can be set in the New Document category of the Dreamweaver Preferences and it is worth keeping this as XHTML as it will give the file a certain degree of future-proofing.

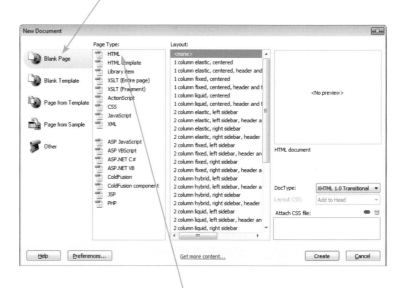

3 Select the type of document you want to create

4 Click Create

5 A new document is opened and its type is displayed in the address bar

Dw Adobe Dreamweaver CS3 - [Untitled-1 (XHTML)]

22

Page-design templates

One of the options when creating new pages is to use one of the page designs that have already been stored within Dreamweaver CS3. This can be a good way to quickly create the basis of professionally designed Web pages. To use page-design templates:

1 Select File, New from the menu bar

2 Click on the Blank Page tab

3 Select a Page Type and the design you want to use

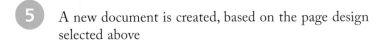

4 Click Create

5 A new document is created, based on the page design selected above

23

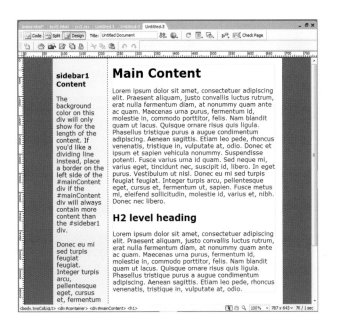

Moving around pages

Because of the power and sophistication of Dreamweaver, page designs can quickly become very involved and complex. Because of this it is useful to be able to move around pages and also zoom in to specific sections of them to see the design in close-up. This can help you create pages as accurately as possible. To do this:

 Open a file. By default this will be displayed at 1:1 size, i.e. 100%

 Select the tools here for moving around the page

3 Click the Hand tool to move around the page

 100% ∨

4 Click here and click on a page to increase the magnification

 200% ∨

5 Click here and select a specific magnification level

6 Once the magnification has been increased, pages can be viewed in greater detail

Using guides

For some aspects of web design, considerable precision is required for positioning objects. This is particularly true when using style sheets (CSS) for formatting and layout purposes, where objects can be positioned at exact points on the page. To help with this, guides can be placed on the page to position objects with pixel-precise accuracy. Guides are not visible when the completed web page is published. To use guides:

1 Select View, Guides, Show Guides from the menu bar

2 Position the cursor over a horizontal or vertical ruler and drag a guide onto the page

3 Hover over a guide on the page to see its exact location, in pixels

4 Guides can be used to create complex grids, which can then be used as a basis for the page content

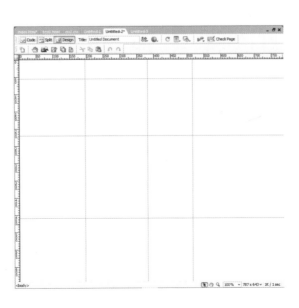

Don't forget

For a detailed look at CSS, and how to use them for formatting and layout purposes, see Chapters 5 and 6.

Hot tip

To view rulers on a page, select View, Rulers, Show from the menu bar.

Accessibility

Accessibility options

An increasingly important issue for websites and web designers is the one of accessibility. This concerns the use of the Web by blind or partially sighted users. Despite the visual nature of the Web, this group of users can still access the information by using a technology that reads the content on screen. This means that someone who is blind or partially sighted is provided with an audio version of websites, rather than just a visual one.

Dreamweaver CS3 enables you to add accessibility features to web pages as they are being created. To do this:

Don't forget

The accessibility guidelines used by Dreamweaver CS3 are based on those contained in Section 508 of the USA's 1998 Rehabilitation Act.

1 Select Edit, Preferences from the menu bar and click Accessibility

2 Check the items that you want to have accessibility features applied to

3 Click OK

Don't forget

Two websites to look at for more information about accessibility issues are the Section 508 site at www.section508.gov and the Web Accessibility Initiative (WAI) at www.w3.org/wai.

4 Whenever one of the elements checked above is added to a web page, a dialog box appears in which you can add the appropriate accessibility features:

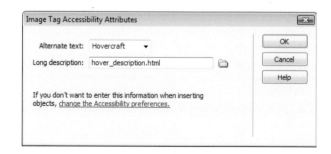

Checking accessibility

In addition to adding accessibility features to elements of a web page, Dreamweaver CS3 also provides a function for checking a site to see if it meets standard accessibility guidelines. To check a site for accessibility compliance:

1 Select File, Check Page, Accessibility from the menu bar

Don't forget

In an accessibility report, an item with a red cross next to it is one that breaches some aspect of the accessibility guidelines; an item with a question mark next to it is one that could cause some confusion for an accessibility reader when it is trying to interpret the page.

27

2 An accessibility report is generated automatically, with a description for each item

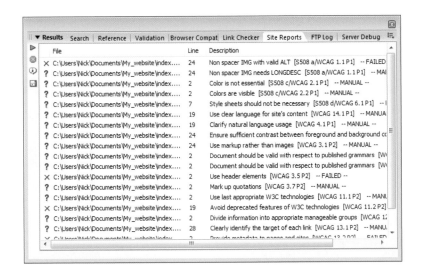

Hot tip

One website that can give reports on the accessibility of a site is Bobby at http://bobby. watchfire.com/bobby.

Getting help

In common with most software programs, Dreamweaver offers an extensive range of help items. These include a general help index, online demonstrations of using the program and websites for the latest upgrades.

Dreamweaver Help

The main help index is displayed in a browser window. This has a variety of options, all of which are accessed from the Help button on the menu bar:

1 Select Help, Dreamweaver Help from the menu bar and select a topic

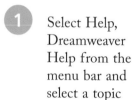

Reference panel

The Reference panel is a help feature provided by the respected publishers O'Reilly. It provides detailed information about the selected item on the page:

1 Select Window, Reference from the menu bar to access the Reference panel

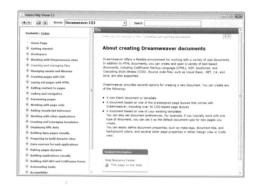

2 Click here to access additional Reference categories

2 Setting up a site

This chapter looks at setting up a site structure into which all of your page content will be placed.

Planning a site

Websites that are published on the Internet are not just random pages that are thrown together in the hope that people will be able to view them over the Web. Instead, each site is a group of pages, images and, if applicable, multimedia effects, linked together by a structure that is invariably created before any of the pages are created. It is possible to create web pages outside a web structure in Dreamweaver and store them on your own computer. However, when it comes to creating a whole site it is important that you create a structure into which you can place all of the content for your site. When it comes to publishing your website on the Internet, you would encounter numerous problems if you had not already set up a site structure.

Preparing a structure

Before you start working with the site-structure tools in Dreamweaver, it is a good idea to decide where you want to store your sites on your own hard drive. The pages and other content for a website are stored in a folder on your hard drive in exactly the same way as any other files. It is therefore a good idea to create a new folder for all of your web authoring files. As you create sites, you can create sub-folders from the main folder for each new site. Also, for each site you may want to create sub-folders for all of the images and so on in your site. If you do this before you start creating your web pages, it will make it easier to save pages and add pages to a site. Once you have set up your folder structure it could look something like this:

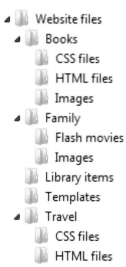

Beware

Do not create a new site in an existing folder that has other files in it. If you do, Dreamweaver will include all of these files in your site structure, even if they are not appropriate.

Hot tip

Draw a rough sketch of your proposed site structure before you start creating folders and files. This does not have to be the definitive structure, but it will give you a good overview of what you are trying to achieve.

Creating a new site

After you have created a folder structure for your websites, you can begin to create individual sites within Dreamweaver. Once a site has been created, the content can then be added and built upon. If all of the items are stored within the same site structure you will be able to perform a variety of site-management tasks with Dreamweaver. Within Dreamweaver CS3 there are options for Basic and Advanced methods of setting up sites. Both of them arrive at the same end result, but the Basic method guides you through the process with a wizard.

Basic site definition

1 Select Site, Manage Sites, New, Site from the menu bar and click the Basic tab

2 Enter a name for the site. Click Next

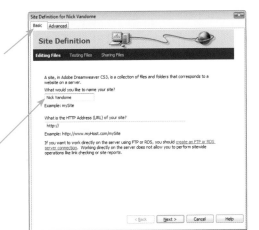

3 Choose this option, unless you want to use server technology. Click Next

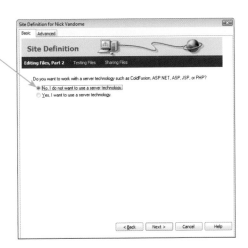

Don't forget

You can create as many structures for different websites as you like. But make sure each one has its own root folder.

Hot tip

Try and give your sites easily identifiable names, rather than just MySite or Website. If you are going to be creating a lot of websites, this is particularly important so that you can quickly identify which is which.

...cont'd

4 Choose this option to edit your files on your own computer before they are published

5 Click here to browse to a folder for storing your local files. Click Next

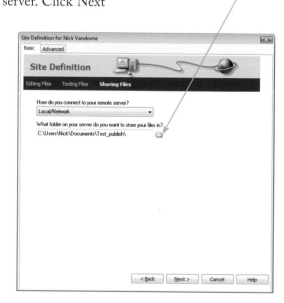

6 Click here to select the location of the remote server, i.e. where your files are going to be published to. Select Local/Network to experiment by publishing them on your own computer. Select FTP to publish them to a remote server. Click Next

Don't forget

For more information on publishing via FTP see Chapter 12.

7 Choose this option (unless you are working in a shared environment, i.e. one in which several people are editing the files within a single site). Click Next

Don't forget

Checking files in and out is used when a team is working on a website and it is necessary to be aware of which files are being edited at any one time. For more information on this, see Chapter 12.

33

8 The final page gives a summary of the selections you have made. Click on Done to close the Site Definition window or Back to change the details

...cont'd

Advanced site definition

1 Select Site, New Site from the menu bar and click the Advanced tab

2 Enter the name for the new site

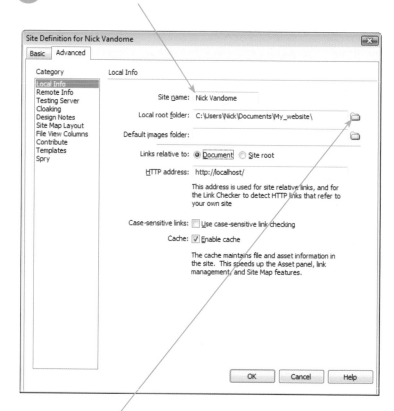

34

3 Click here to browse your hard drive for the folder in which the new site will be stored. This is known as the root folder for the site

4 Click OK

Setting up a home page

Every website has to have a home page. This is the one that appears when the site is first accessed and, as far as the browser viewing the site is concerned, everything within the site is created relative to the home page. This can be particularly important when you are performing certain site-management tasks, because Dreamweaver needs to know which is the home page, to use this as a reference point. There are two ways to define a home page in Dreamweaver.

From the Site Definition window
The home page can be specified in the Site Definition window when a site is first defined or it can be edited once the site has been created. Either way, the process for specifying the home page is the same:

Hot tip

Name the home page in each Dreamweaver site "index.htm" or "index.html". They can be given other names, but these are the ones that work most effectively within Dreamweaver.

1 Select Site Map Layout in the Site Definition window

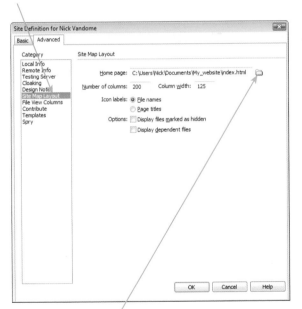

To retrieve this window,
Site → Manage Sites →
Click on the site name →
Edit.

Don't forget

The Site Definition window can be accessed from either Design view or the Site panel. For both, select Site, Manage Sites, New, Site from the menu bar to create a new site. To edit an existing site, select Site, Manage Sites from the menu bar, select the site you want to edit and select Edit.

2 Click here to browse for a home page in the Choose Home Page dialog box. Select a file and click Open

3 Click OK

...cont'd

From the Site panel

1 Click on the Files panel and select a file from the local directory

2 Click here and select Site

Don't forget

Get into the habit of creating and naming a home page at the same time as any new sites are created.

36

Hot tip

You can also set the home page by right-clicking (Windows) or Ctrl+clicking (Mac) on a file in the Site panel and selecting Set as Home Page from the menu.

3 Select Set as Home Page from the Site menu

Viewing the site map

The site map is a website-management tool that displays a graphical representation of all of the files in the current site and the way that they relate to each other. Each file in the site map is defined in relation to the home page. This is one reason why it is important to specify a home page. The site map shows the links between various files within the current site and also any files that have broken links. To access the site map:

1 Click here in the Files panel and select Map View

Don't forget

To return to File view, select Local View from the drop-down menu in the Files panel.

37

2 Click here to expand and collapse the Files panel

3 Click here to view the site map and the local files

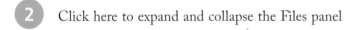

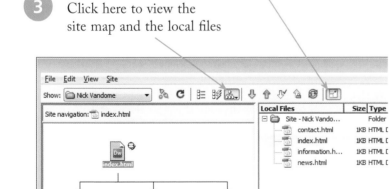

100%   1 local items selected totalling 511 bytes.

Hot tip

New files and folders can be added to a site by clicking on the File menu in the Files panel and selecting New File or New Folder.

Defining a site

A site can be defined when it is first created, and it is also possible to change these settings once a site has been set up. To create or edit the definition of a site:

Don't forget

Other categories in the Site Definition box include: Remote Info, which covers aspects of publishing a site and is looked at in more detail in Chapter 12; Testing Server, which is used with dynamic web pages, and is looked at in Chapter 11; and Cloaking, which can be used to prevent certain files being published, and is looked at in more detail in Chapter 12.

38

 Click here in the Files panel and select Site, Manage Sites

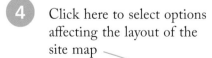 Select a site and click on Edit

Hot tip

Design Notes is a function that allows designers to add notes to web pages as they are working on them. This can be particularly useful if several designers are working on the same site.

3 Click here to select the options for using Design Notes within a site

4 Click here to select options affecting the layout of the site map

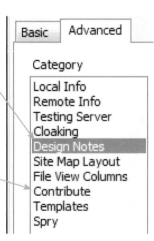

3 Editing HTML

This chapter looks at the options that Dreamweaver provides for adding and editing HTML (Hypertext Markup Language) code, which is used to create web pages. It shows how to create your own code and covers some of the features that assist in the process and help to speed it up. It also shows how to import content from Word and Excel documents.

HTML overview

Hypertext Markup Language (HTML) is the computer code used to create web pages. It is not a fully-blown computer-programming language, but rather a set of instructions that enables a web browser to determine the layout of pages.

HTML is created by using a series of tags, which contain the instructions that are interpreted by the browsers. These tags are placed around the item to which you want that particular command to apply. Most tags, but not all of them, have an opening and a closing element. The opening tag contains the particular command and the closing tag contains the same command, but with a "/" in front of it to denote the end of the command. For instance, if you wanted to display a piece of text as bold, you could do it with the following piece of HTML:

This text would appear bold in a browser

HTML is a text-based code, which means that the source HTML file only contains text and not any images or multimedia items. These appear in the browser because of a reference to them that is placed in an HTML document. For instance, if you wanted to include an image in a document you would insert the following piece of HTML into your source file:

<img src="myimage.jpg">

This would instruct the browser to insert this image at the required point within the HTML document when it is being viewed on the Web. It is possible to insert HTML code to call for a variety of graphics and multimedia files to be displayed in a web page. However, it is important to remember that when you are publishing your pages, all of the items that are referred to in the source HTML document are uploaded to the server as well as the HTML file.

Since Dreamweaver is a "what you see is what you get" (WYSIWYG) program, it generates all of the HTML in the background. This means that it is possible to ignore the HTML's existence completely. However, it is useful to learn the basics.

Common tags

Unless otherwise stated, tags have an equivalent closing tag, created by inserting "/" in front of the command. Some of the most commonly used tags in HTML are:

- <p> This creates a new paragraph

- <strong> This creates bold text

- <em> This creates italics

- <u> This creates underlined text

-
  This inserts a line break (this does not have a closing tag)

- <hr> This inserts a horizontal line (this does not have a closing tag)

- <img src="image.jpg"> This inserts the specified image (this does not have a closing tag)

- <font face="Arial"> This specifies a certain font. The closing tag is just </font>

- <h1> This formats text at a preset heading size. There are six levels for this, "h1" being the largest and "h6" being the smallest. Paragraph and other formatting tags cannot be used within heading tags

- <table> This inserts a table

- <color="ffffff"> This can be used to select a color for a variety of items, including background color and text color

- <a href="default.htm">Home Page</a> This is used to create a hyperlink to another web page. In this case the link is to the file "default.htm" and the words "Home Page" will appear underlined on the web page, denoting that it is a link to another page

Beware

Underlined text should only be used as a design feature on web pages in exceptional circumstances. This is because hyperlinks (the device used to move to other pages and websites) usually appear underlined to denote their status. If normal text is also underlined, this could cause confusion.

Don't forget

If you are using CSS for formatting text the <font> tag should not be used in the HTML document. In these cases, it is known as a deprecated tag.

Page views

Although it is possible to be blissfully unaware of the existence of HTML when you are using Dreamweaver, you can also hand-code pages using Code view. This allows you to create your own HTML code, which is then translated into the document window by Dreamweaver. This can be a good way to learn about HTML and perform fine-tuning tasks if you cannot achieve the result you want through the document window. In Dreamweaver CS3 you can access the graphical version of the page, the HTML code on its own or a combination of them both:

Don't forget

When Code view and Design view are showing together, if any changes are made in one of these views the other is updated automatically.

Click here to access Code and Design view together

Click here to access Design view on its own

Click here to access the Code view on its own

HTML preferences

Code colors

When creating and editing HTML within Dreamweaver, it is possible to set various defaults for the colors within the HTML Source window. This can be useful not only for aesthetic reasons, but also to make specific elements stand out within the code. These elements can then be quickly identified when working with the source code. To set the preferences for colors within the HTML Source window:

Don't forget

Use a consistent theme for colors within the HTML Source window, so that you can easily recognize different elements within the code even if you are working on different websites.

1. Select Edit, Preferences from the menu bar

2. Select Code Coloring in the Preferences dialog box

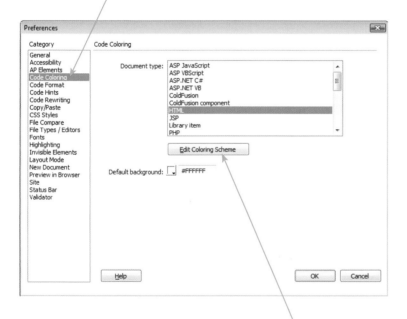

Don't forget

As with all of the color palettes within Dreamweaver, it is possible to apply a wider range of colors for the HTML options than the ones on the standard palette that appears. Click on the paint palette at the bottom-right corner to create your own custom colors.

3. Click here to edit the existing color scheme

4. Click OK

...cont'd

The options for setting colors for code coloring are:

- Background. This affects the background color of the window

- Text. This affects the color of the text that appears in the document

- Bold, italic and underlining

Hot tip

One of the most versatile ways of aligning and laying out images and text is through the use of tables. This will enable you to produce precision alignment. The alignment options on this page can also be applied to images and text once they are inserted into a table. For more on tables, see Chapter 8.

Select a tag from this list

Click here to select a font color

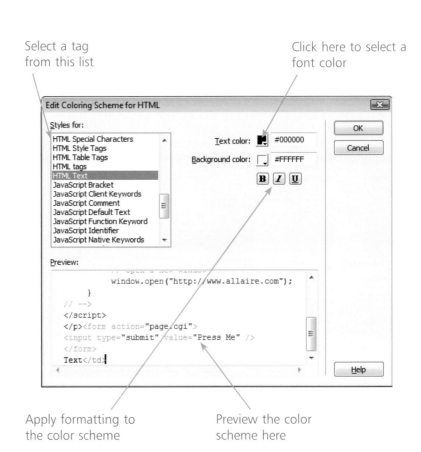

Apply formatting to the color scheme

Preview the color scheme here

Code format

These preferences can be used to determine the layout of the code within the HTML Source window. These include the way tags are presented and also the use of indents and tabs to indicate certain elements, such as tables and frames. To access the Code Format preferences:

Select Code Format from the Preferences dialog box

Click here to specify how indents are displayed and which items will appear indented

Don't forget

According to the values that are set, different elements on a page will be displayed with code that is indented in the HTML source. For instance, the code for table rows and columns and frames is usually indented.

Enter tab values

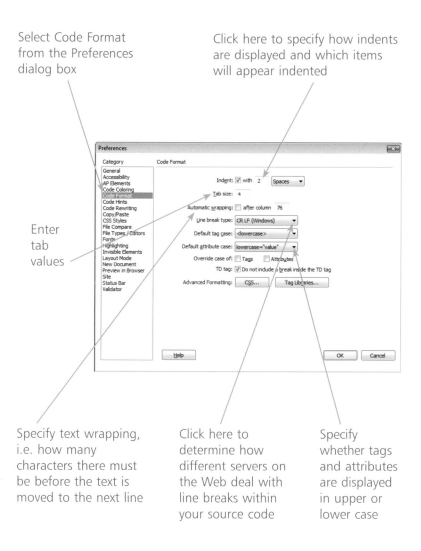

45

Beware

Specify text wrapping, i.e. how many characters there must be before the text is moved to the next line

Click here to determine how different servers on the Web deal with line breaks within your source code

Specify whether tags and attributes are displayed in upper or lower case

Before you start creating web pages, decide whether you want your tags to be in upper or lower case. Once you have done this, stick to it for all of your pages and sites, for the sake of consistency. In general, lower-case tags are neater and take up less space in the code.

Coding toolbar

In Code view there is a toolbar to help with entering and editing HTML code. The elements of this are:

46

Open documents (displays currently open files)

 Collapse full tag

Collapse selection

 Expand all

Select parent tag

 Balance braces

Show or hide line numbers

 Highlight invalid code

Apply comment

 Remove comment

Wrap tag

 Recent snippets

Move or convert CSS

 Indent code

Outdent code

 Format source code

Collapsing code

When working in Code view it is sometimes useful to be able to collapse sections of code so that work can be done on other elements of the code. There are various ways in which this can be done within Code view:

1 Click here on the Coding toolbar to display line numbers next to the code

2 Select a tag in the code and click next to the line number to select the whole tag

3 Click on the minus sign to collapse the code

4 Click on the plus sign to expand the code

5 Highlight a block of code and click here to collapse the selection

6 Use the Code toolbar to expand and collapse selections:

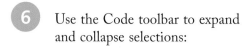

Collapse the whole of a selected tag

Collapse selected code

Expand all of the code

Select the parent tag of a selection

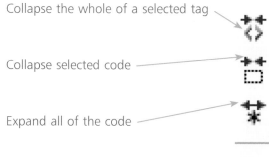

47

Hot tip

If you are working in Code view, collapsing portions of the code that you are not working on can be a good way to make the code look less cluttered and less daunting to work with.

Don't forget

A parent tag is the dominant one in a group of nested tags. For instance, in a table the main <table> tag is the parent one and the <tr> tags (table rows) are the child tags. Similarly, a <td> tag (table cell) is the child tag to the relevant <tr> tag, which is the parent.

Tag Chooser

To speed up the process of creating HTML, Dreamweaver has a number of functions for inserting HTML tags or blocks of code, rather than having to create it all by hand. One of these is the Tag Chooser, where HTML tags can be inserted with a couple of mouse clicks. To do this:

Hot tip

Once the Insert button is clicked in the Tag Chooser dialog box the selected tag is entered into Code view but the dialog box remains visible until Close is clicked. Therefore keep the Code view window visible so that you can see when the code has been added. This means that you can add several tags without having to activate the Tag Chooser dialog box each time.

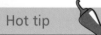

Hot tip

Some tags have additional properties that can be added in a dialog box once the tag has been selected.

48

1 Insert the cursor in Code view, at the point where you want the tag to appear

```
74    </table>
75    <p> </p>
76    </div>
77    |
78    </body>
79    </html>
```

2 Right-click (Windows) or Ctrl+click (Mac) and select Insert Tag

3 In the Tag Chooser window select the tag you want to use and click Insert

4 The tag is inserted into the document at the insertion point

```
75    <p> </p>
76    </div>
77    <hr align="center" width="100" size="2">
78    </body>
79    </html>
```

Tag Libraries

The tags that appear in the Tag Chooser are stored in the Tag Library. It is possible to add tags to the Tag Library and also edit existing ones. This gives increased versatility for the HTML tags at your disposal. To edit tags in the Tag Library:

1   Select Edit, Tag Libraries from the menu bar

2   Select a tag to view its attributes and edit them as required

3   Click here to create a new library for your own tags or to create new tags. Click OK

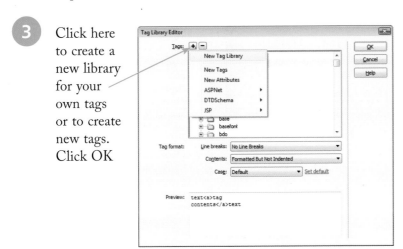

Hot tip

You may want to create new Tag Libraries and tags if you are using a server technology such as Active Server Pages or ColdFusion.

49

4   For a new Tag Library, enter a name and click OK

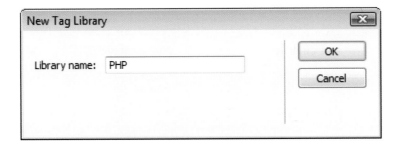

Tag Inspector

The Tag Inspector is a panel that enables you to see the attributes for a selected item, and amend them if required. To use the Tag Inspector:

1 Select an item to view its properties in the Tag Inspector

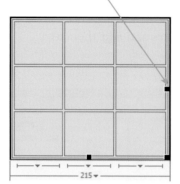

50

2 Select an attribute and enter details here to change its parameters

3 The changes in the Tag Inspector will be applied to the selected object

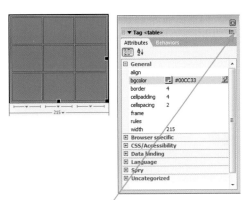

4 Click here and select Edit Tag

5 Enter new parameters for the tag in the Tag Editor

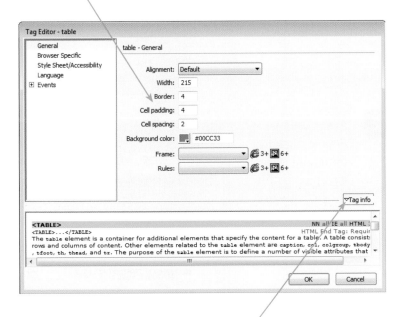

6 Click here to view reference information about the selected tag

7 Click OK

Beware

Once a change has been made to a tag in the Tag Editor, this only applies to the selected item. It does not apply to any similar items that are subsequently created.

51

Code snippets

One of the new features of Dreamweaver CS3 is the ability to add blocks, or snippets, of HTML code into documents. This is done with the Snippets panel, and existing snippets can be used as well as creating new ones. To use the Snippets panel:

1 Click the Snippets tab to view the current Snippets folders

2 Select a folder by double-clicking on it, and select a snippet within it by clicking on it once

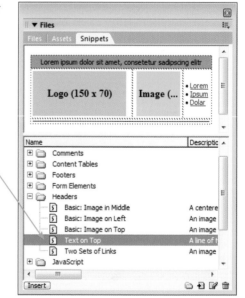

3 Click Insert

4 The selected snippet of code is inserted into the current document. Depending on the type of snippet, it will be displayed in Design view and Code view. However, some snippets, such as metadata, will only be displayed in Code view

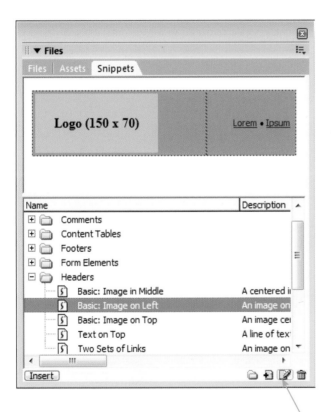

5 To edit an existing snippet, select it in the Snippets panel and click here

Don't forget

Metadata are contained within the <head> tag of an HTML page, and they store items such as keywords and descriptions about a page, which can be used by search engines trying to locate the page. Metadata can also include items such as information about how frequently a page should be automatically refreshed by the browser, if required.

Hot tip

A lot of snippets that follow accessibility guidelines can be found in the Accessible folder.

...cont'd

6 The code that makes up the snippet is displayed in the Snippet dialog box

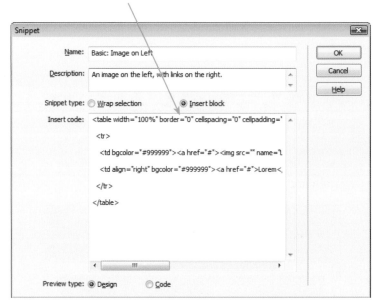

7 Make any changes that are required and click OK

Creating new snippets

1 Click here in the Snippets panel to create a new snippets folder

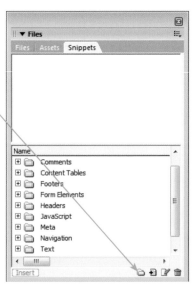

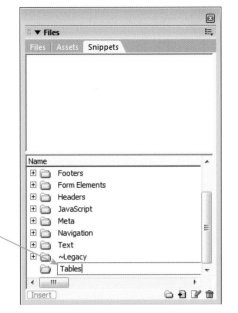

2 Enter a name for the new snippets folder

3 Select an object or a piece of HTML code

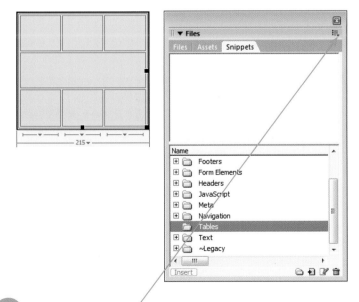

4 Click here to select the Snippets panel menu and then select New Snippet

...cont'd

5 The code for the snippet is already inserted. Enter a name and description for the snippet and, if necessary, amend the code

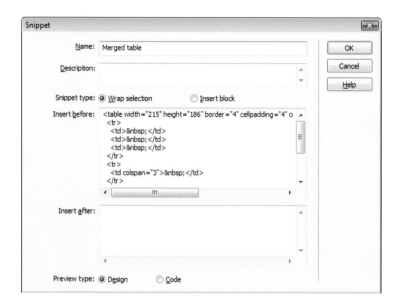

Don't forget

The preview type can be set to Design or Code. This determines how the snippet is displayed in the Preview panel of the Snippets panel. Design gives a graphical preview and Code displays the HTML code.

6 Click OK

7 The new snippet is added to the new folder in the Snippets panel and can now be used in the same way as any other snippet

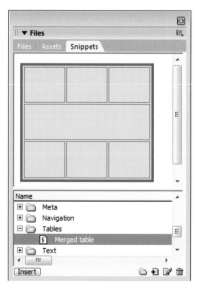

Invalid code

If you write any invalid code in the Code view, or turn off all of the HTML Rewriting preferences when opening a document from another source, any invalid code will be highlighted in yellow, in both the Code-view window and the Design-view window. This means that Dreamweaver has encountered some code that it does not understand, and therefore it cannot display it correctly or reformat it automatically. However, it is possible to manually correct any invalid code:

1 Click on the tags that denote invalid HTML code. This can be done either in the Code-view window or in Design view

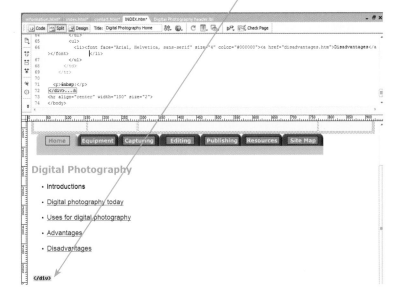

2 A window will appear alerting you to the reasons for the invalid code and instructing you how to repair it. Follow these instructions and check that the invalid code tags have subsequently disappeared

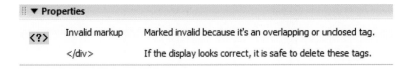

Don't forget

On occasions, a whole string of HTML tags will be marked as being invalid. However, this can sometimes be corrected by fixing one tag, for example by changing its nesting order.

Hot tip

If you are familiar with HTML, it can be quicker to fix invalid code in the Code-view window than in Design view.

57

Don't forget

If you encounter any invalid code on your pages, press F12 to see how this affects the page when it is viewed in a browser. In some cases it will be unnoticeable.

Quick Tag Editor

When editing HTML code there will probably be times when you want to quickly change or add a specific tag. This can be done by accessing Code view. However, it is also possible to do this without leaving Design view, through the use of the Quick Tag Editor. This is a function that enables you to insert and check HTML tags directly in the Design-view window. Any changes that are made are updated automatically in the Code-view window. The Quick Tag Editor can be accessed by selecting Modify, Quick Tag Editor from the menu bar or by using Ctrl+T (Windows) or Command+T (Mac). This shortcut can also be used to toggle between the different modes of the Quick Tag Editor.

There are two different modes that can be used within the Quick Tag Editor:

Insert HTML mode

This enables you to insert new HTML tags into a document. If required, it can be used to insert a string of several tags together. If the closing tags are not inserted, then Dreamweaver will place these automatically in the most appropriate place.

58

1. Insert the cursor at the point where you want to create a new HTML tag. Do not select any elements on the page

Uses for digital photography

2. Press Ctrl+T (Windows) or Command+T (Mac) and enter the required tag and any content. If you wait a couple of seconds a drop-down hints menu will appear with a choice of tags to use

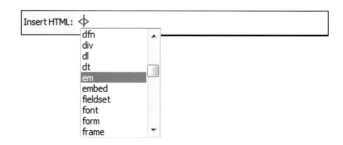

Edit Tag mode

This can be used to edit existing HTML tags in a document. The Quick Tag Editor opens in this mode if an item with an opening and closing tag is selected on the page.

1 Select an element on the page that contains an opening tag, content and a closing tag. This could mean selecting an image, or an entire section of formatted text

2 Press Ctrl+T (Windows) or Command+T (Mac) to open the Quick Tag Editor in Edit Tag mode

```
Edit tag: <img src="scott_monument4.jpg"
          alt="Monument" width="200" height="244"
          hspace="6" border="0">
```

3 Edit the tag and then apply the changes by clicking back in the Design-view window

```
Edit tag: <img src="scott_monument4.jpg"
          alt="Monument" width="400" height="488"
          hspace="6" border="0">
```

4 If you enter an incorrect tag, you will be alerted to this by a warning dialog box

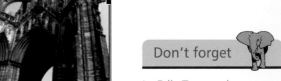

Don't forget

In Edit Tag mode, you can edit tags manually, i.e. write the HTML tags yourself, or insert a new tag from the hints menu that appears after a couple of seconds.

Selecting and removing tags

Selecting tags

In addition to selecting tags with the Quick Tag Editor by selecting items in the document window, it is also possible to select them from the tag selector, which is located at the bottom-left of the document window. This enables you to easily identify the opening and closing tags and also the content that is contained within them. To select tags using the tag selector:

Don't forget

The Quick Tag Editor is a good way to ensure that you select specific tags accurately within the HTML code.

Don't forget

Some tags appear in the tag selector when items are selected by clicking on them in the document window. Others, such as the "body" tag, are always visible.

1 The relevant tags are displayed in the tag selector, which is located at the bottom-left of the document window

`<body> <tr> <td> <p> <img>`

2 Select a tag by clicking on it once. The equivalent item is highlighted in the document window. This can then be edited using the Quick Tag Editor

Removing tags

Right-click (Windows) or Ctrl+click (Mac) on one of the tags in the tag selector and select Remove Tag from the contextual menu.

Hot tip

The tags displayed in the tag selector can also be used to access the Quick Tag Edit mode. To do this, right-click (Windows) or Ctrl+click (Mac) on the required tag in the tag selector; the Quick Tag Editor will open in Edit mode, using the selected tag.

Remove Tag
Quick Tag Editor...
Set Class
Set ID
Convert Inline CSS to Rule...
Collapse Full Tag
Collapse Outside Full Tag

Adding HTML text

When dealing with text, at least initially, it can be easier for
formatting to use HTML tags rather than CSS ones. To ensure
this, open the Preferences window and click on the General
Preferences option. Under "Editing options", make sure the "Use
CSS instead of HTML tags" box is not checked:

Editing options: ☑ Show dialog when inserting objects
☑ Enable double-byte inline input
☑ Switch to plain paragraph after heading
☐ Allow multiple consecutive spaces
☑ Use <strong> and <em> in place of <b> and <i>
☐ Use CSS instead of HTML tags

Whenever text is being added, or edited, the Text Properties
Inspector is displayed. This shows the attributes of the current
piece of text and it can be used to perform a variety of text-
formatting tasks:

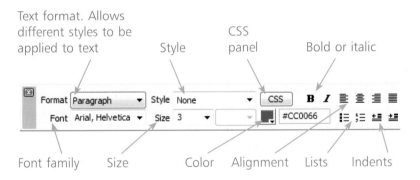

Text format. Allows different styles to be applied to text — Style — CSS panel — Bold or italic

Font family — Size — Color — Alignment — Lists — Indents

A lot of these commands can also be selected from the Text
option on the menu bar and from the Text tab on the
Insert panel.

Don't forget

CSS stands for
"cascading style sheet"
and is a device for
creating customized
formatting for HTML
documents. For more
information on this, see
Chapters 5 and 6.

Don't forget

If the Text Properties
Inspector is not showing
when you insert or edit
text, select Window,
Properties from the
menu bar.

Pasting from Word and Excel

When creating web pages a lot of the content is taken from existing sources, two of the most common being Word and Excel. In some previous versions of Dreamweaver it was possible to copy and paste content from these applications, but most of the formatting was lost in the process. However, with Dreamweaver CS3 it is possible to import content from Word and Excel and keep the original formatting intact. The process is the same for both Word and Excel documents.

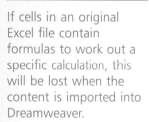

Beware

Always check the pasted content to make sure the formatting is the same as in the original. In some cases, minor editing may be required.

1 Select a piece of text in a Word or an Excel document and copy it

2 Open a new Dreamweaver document and select Edit, Paste Formatted from the menu bar to import the formatted content

Beware

If cells in an original Excel file contain formulas to work out a specific calculation, this will be lost when the content is imported into Dreamweaver.

3 Select the formatting options for pasting the text and click OK

4 The content is pasted into Dreamweaver with its original formatting intact

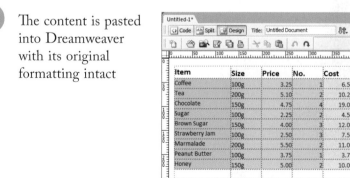

4 Working with images

This chapter gives an overview of using images on the Web and explains how to use and edit them in Dreamweaver, including editing them with Photoshop.

Web image overview

When the Web was first being developed it was considered to be a significant achievement to transfer plain, unformatted text from one computer to another. However, things have moved on considerably from then and the Web is now awash with complex graphics, animations and sounds, to name but a few of the multimedia effects that are now available to the web designer.

Despite the range of items that can be used on web pages, graphics are still by far the most popular. These can include photographic images, icons, clip art and even animated graphics. These are all important design elements for web pages and they should not be overlooked when you are creating a new website.

When graphical formats were being developed for the Web there was a need to create good-quality images that were still small enough to allow them to be downloaded quickly onto the user's computer. This resulted in two file formats that offer good quality while still creating small file sizes. These are Graphics Interchange Format (GIF) and Joint Photographic Experts Group (JPEG). Some points to bear in mind about both of these formats:

- JPEGs use up to 16 million colors and so are best suited for photographic images

- GIFs use 256 colors and so are best suited for images that do not contain a lot of color definition, such as images with blocks of similar color

- One variety of GIF (GIF 89a) can be used to create images with transparent backgrounds

- Both GIFs and JPEGs use forms of compression to make the file size smaller

Another, more recent, image format for the Web is PNG (Portable Network Graphics). It uses 16 million colors and lossless compression. There are a couple of points to consider with PNGs:

- Not all browsers support the PNG format

- PNG files can contain metatags, indexing information that can be read by web search engines when someone is looking for your website

Using images effectively

When you use a program such as Dreamweaver, which gives you the power to quickly and easily insert images into web pages, the temptation is to add them at every opportunity. However, this should be resisted as it is important to use images carefully and make the most of their impact and design potential. Some points to bear in mind when using images on web pages are:

- The more images you include, the longer it will take for the user to download your site, i.e. to access it from the host server. This can cause a real problem, because most web users do not have the patience to wait a long time for pages to download. This can be measured in seconds rather than minutes

- Images can be used as the background to a web page or as independent items within it. Either way, the file size of the image will determine the downloading time

- Keep the on-screen size of images small. Again, this can affect the downloading time and it can detract from other content on a page

- Do not overuse images that spin, blink or flicker. While this can create a positive initial effect, it can become extremely irritating after it has been viewed several times

- Use images for a specific purpose, i.e. to convey information or as a design feature

- Do not use images that could be deemed offensive or derogatory to any individuals or groups

- Use the same image, or groups of images, to achieve a consistent look throughout a website

- Do not use images just for the sake of it, or just because you can. Users will soon realize that the images are not serving a useful purpose

- Do not use images at the expense of core information. Users may want to find a piece of contact information rather than look at a lot of images

Beware

Do not make your website too dependent on images, since users can set their browsers so that they do not display any graphics.

Inserting images

Obtaining images

Images for insertion in a website can be obtained from a variety of sources:

Don't forget

For a detailed look at digital cameras and digital images, take a look at "Digital Photography in Easy Steps" in this series.

- System clip-art collections. Most computers come with some items of clip art already pre-installed

- CD-ROMs. There are several CD-ROMs on the market that contain tens of thousands of graphical and photographic images

- Digital cameras. These are affordable for the home user and offer a versatile option for creating your own images for a web page

- Scanners. These can be used to capture existing images in a digital format

Inserting images

Hot tip

To use an image for the background of a page, select Modify, Page Properties from the menu bar. Click on the Browse button next to the Background Image box and select an image in the same way as for inserting it directly onto a page. To create a watermark effect, use an image-editing program to make the image semi-transparent and then insert it as the background.

1 Insert the cursor at the point on the page where you want the image and click on the Image button on the Common tab of the Insert panel

2 Locate the image you want to use and click on OK (Windows) or Choose (Mac)

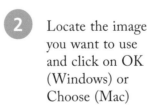

Image properties

When an image is selected in Dreamweaver, the Properties Inspector displays information about that image. To access the Image Properties Inspector:

1 Select an image by clicking on it once

2 The Image Properties Inspector is activated

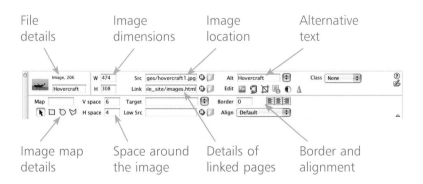

File details

Image dimensions

Image location

Alternative text

Image map details

Space around the image

Details of linked pages

Border and alignment

Don't forget

When an image is inserted on a page in Dreamweaver, it only really inserts a reference to where the image is located on your computer, rather than the image itself being physically inserted. This reference is denoted by the <src> tag.

Don't forget

Using alternative ("alt") text in place of an image is important for people who choose not to view images or who are visually impaired and use a reader to view the Web. Type a description of the image in the Alt box. This can be a couple of words or several sentences.

Aligning images and text

During the process of creating a website, there will be several occasions when you will want to combine images and text. This could be to include a textual definition of an image or to wrap a block of text around an image, in the style of a newspaper or a magazine article. This can be done through the use of various Dreamweaver functions (see the margin note), or an image can have a value assigned to it so that it deals with text alignment in a certain way. To align an image and text together:

1 Select an image by clicking on it once. It may already have text around it, or the text can be added later:

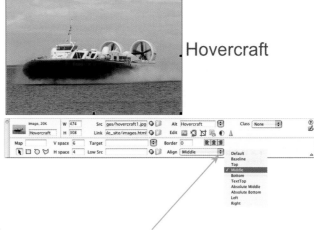

Hovercraft

2 Click here to access the various alignment options

Don't forget

The baseline of a text block is the line on which the bottom of most of the letters sit. This does not include descenders (such as in "g" and "j"), which extend below the baseline.

The options for aligning images and text are:

- Default. This varies between browsers but it usually aligns the text baseline with the image base

- Baseline. This aligns the baseline with the image base

- Top. This aligns the tallest point of the text with the top of the image

- Middle. This aligns the text baseline with the middle of the image

- Bottom. This aligns the baseline of the text with the bottom of the image

- TextTop. This aligns the tallest point of the text with the top of the image (it usually produces the same effect as Top)

- Absolute Middle. This aligns the middle of the text block with the middle of the image

- Absolute Bottom. This aligns the bottom of the text, including descenders, with the bottom of the image

- Left. This places the image to the left of any text that is next to it. The text will then wrap around the image

- Right. This places the image to the right of any text that is next to it

Alignment buttons

As well as using the alignment options described above, it is also possible to align images and text by using the alignment buttons in the Image Properties Inspector. Even though this is done by selecting an image, the alignment is applied to the text:

Image with the Left alignment option or the Align Left button

Bouncy castle

Image with the Middle alignment option or the Align Center button

Bouncy castle

Beware

Aligning images and text can create some interesting, and sometimes unwanted, effects. Experiment with different settings until you feel confident about each combination.

Don't forget

Another use for images is the "trace" option. This is where a design has been created and is then inserted onto a web page as a background for the web designer to copy, or trace over. The trace image does not appear on the published page and it is really a guide for the Web designer to follow. To use a trace image, select Modify, Page Properties from the menu bar and in the Tracing Image window select the trace image as you would for any other image. There are also options for applying certain levels of transparency.

Editing images

Since images are an integral part of websites, it is important to be able to edit them as quickly and efficiently as possible, when working within the web authoring environment. Dreamweaver achieves this by allowing one-click access to image-editing programs and also by providing some image-editing functionality within Dreamweaver itself.

Accessing external image editors

 Select an image within Dreamweaver

 Click here to access the image-editing options:

Hot tip

The default image editor is Fireworks, another Adobe product. However, it is possible to change this in the File Types / Editors window within the Preferences panel. Even if another image editor is set as the default, the Fireworks icon will still be displayed in the Properties Inspector.

Don't forget

Sharpening is an image-editing technique that can improve the clarity of images that are slightly blurry. Moderate sharpening can improve most digital images.

Beware

Once image-editing commands have been set within Dreamweaver these are applied to the original image and are permanent. However, the editing can be undone by selecting Edit, Undo from the menu bar.

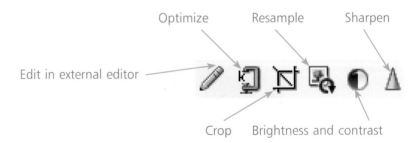

Optimize   Resample   Sharpen

Edit in external editor

Crop   Brightness and contrast

Editing with Photoshop

As far as editing images is concerned, previous versions of Dreamweaver were more closely integrated with Fireworks. But in CS3 the main image-editing functions can now be done in Adobe Photoshop, the most popular image-editing program on the market. It is now possible to import Photoshop files (.psd) into Dreamweaver, optimize them for use on the Web and leave the original master file untouched. To do this:

1 *With the cursor where you want to insert the image* Click on this button in the Common section of the Insert panel

2 Browse to a Photoshop file, i.e. one that has been created with a .psd extension. Select it and click OK (Windows) or Choose (Mac)

3 The Image Preview window enables you to reduce the file size so that the image can be downloaded more quickly over the Web. Click here to reduce the quality of the image, which will also reduce the file size

Hot tip

To ensure that you use Photoshop for all of your image-editing functions, select Edit, Preferences from the menu bar. In the File Types / Editors section click on the Browse button. Navigate to where Photoshop is located on your hard drive and select it. This will make it the primary image-editing program when you are working with images in Dreamweaver.

...cont'd

4 Click on the File tab and enter values in the W and H boxes to reduce the physical size of the image

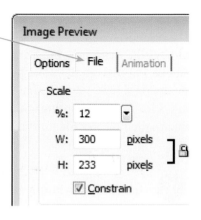

5 Click OK

6 You will be prompted to save the image. This will be done according to the selections in step 3. Give the file a new name and click Save (this ensures that the original file remains untouched)

7 The image is inserted into the Dreamweaver file in an image format and size that is suitable for displaying on the Web

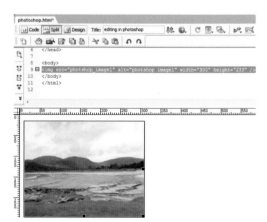

Creating rollover images

One of the most eye-catching effects with images on the Web is the creation of rollovers. This is where two images are combined, although only one is visible initially on the page. However, when the cursor is moved over the image, it is replaced by the second one. To make this even more impressive, a hyperlink can be added to the rollover so that the user can click on it and be taken to another page within the site, or a different site altogether.

Until recently, rollovers were the preserve of designers who could use programming languages such as Javascript. However, Dreamweaver overcomes this by allowing you to create rollovers, while generating all of the script in the background. This means that you have a powerful design tool at your disposal, without having to delve into computer-language scripting.

Creating a rollover image

1 Create the two images that you want to use for the rollover. Make sure they are the same dimensions, because they will be produced as the same size in the rollover

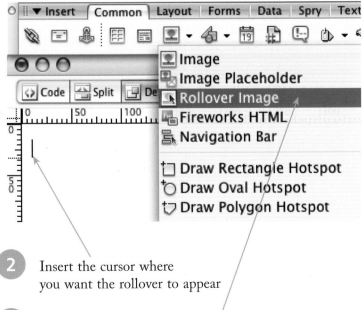

2 Insert the cursor where you want the rollover to appear

3 Select the Rollover Image button on the Insert panel

Beware

Do not get too carried away with using rollovers, although this can be difficult to resist when you first learn how to create them. As with any item on a web page that moves or changes from one thing to another, a little goes a long way.

Hot tip

If you are using a rollover to link to another page or site on the Web, choose your images carefully so that users can quickly relate the image with the link that it contains. Otherwise, they may think that it is just a clever graphical effect.

...cont'd

4 Click here to enter a name for the rollover button

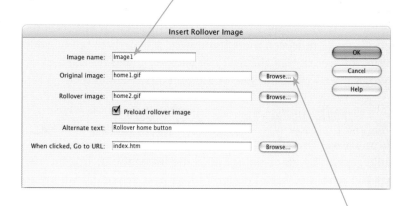

5 Click here to locate the first image you are going to use. Repeat the process by clicking the button below for the second image

6 If you want users to be able to go to another web page when they click, enter a file in the "When clicked, Go to URL" box. Click OK to create the rollover

7 When viewed in a browser, the image will look like this initially...

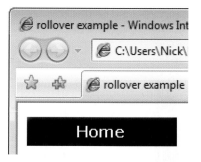

...and this when the cursor moves over it

5 Using CSS

Cascading style sheets (CSS) are sets of rules that can be used to format the content of HTML documents. This chapter introduces the elements of CSS, shows how to create pages with CSS and details how to attach CSS to HTML documents in Dreamweaver.

CSS overview

In the early days of web design the majority of pages were created with HTML code. This specified the content and formatting within the same document. However, this could be cumbersome in that each time there was a change in formatting this would have to be included in the HTML document. For instance, each time a different font was used, this had to be specified in terms of font family, size and color.

In recent years cascading style sheets (CSS) have become a lot more popular for designing web pages. This is because they can be used to separate the content and presentation of web pages. The content is still in the HTML document but the presentation (or formatting) is included within the CSS document in the form of a group of formatting rules. These can then be applied to multiple files. This means that if one of the rules is updated the appearance of the relevant content in all of the linked files is also updated, without the need to edit the individual HTML files. CSS rules can be used for formatting and positioning items.

A CSS rule consists of two parts: the selector and the declaration. The selector refers to the rule that is being created or defined, and the declaration refers to the elements of the rule. CSS styles can be imported directly into an HTML document, in which case they are usually located in the <head> section of the document, or they can be created in specific CSS files. These have a .css extension and can be linked to the HTML document.

Hot tip

For a detailed look at working with cascading style sheets and creating web pages with them, look at "CSS in Easy Steps" in this series.

76

CSS elements

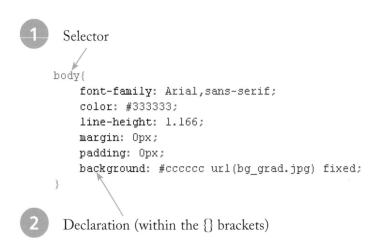

1 Selector

```
body{
    font-family: Arial,sans-serif;
    color: #333333;
    line-height: 1.166;
    margin: 0px;
    padding: 0px;
    background: #cccccc url(bg_grad.jpg) fixed;
}
```

2 Declaration (within the {} brackets)

CSS in Dreamweaver

Dreamweaver CS3 has been developed to maximize the use of style sheets in the creation of web pages and make them as easy to use and manipulate as possible. This is done using the Properties Inspector and the CSS Styles panel:

1 Click here on the Properties Inspector to include specific CSS styles

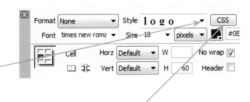

2 Click here to access the CSS Styles panel

3 Use the CSS Styles panel to create, add and edit style sheets. The properties of included style sheets are displayed within this panel

Don't forget

In Dreamweaver CS3 there is more emphasis on using CSS rather than just plain HTML code. However, traditional HTML coding is still catered for, either on its own for content and presentation, or in conjunction with style sheets for formatting.

77

4 Within Design view, complex CSS designs are displayed, even if the CSS rules are contained in a separate .css file

CSS and HTML

Although CSS and HTML are separate, but related, items of a web page, Dreamweaver has an option for working with the emphasis on one option or the other. This affects how some of the code in the HTML document appears. If you are going to be working with CSS there is a preference option for specifying the use of CSS styles rather than HTML tags, where appropriate. To do this:

Don't forget

When using CSS the content for a web page is still contained within the HTML file. The style sheet specifies the appearance of the content.

1 Select Edit, Preferences (Windows) or Dreamweaver, Preferences (Mac) from the menu bar

2 Select the General category

3 Check this box to use CSS styles instead of HTML tags (where appropriate)

4 Click OK

5 In HTML mode, all of the formatting for an element is included within the HTML code of the document

```
12   <p><strong><font color="#CC3366" size="7" face="Arial, Helvetica, sans-serif">Heading</font></strong>
13   </p>
```

Heading

...cont'd

6 If style sheets are being used, the formatting can be included within the tag

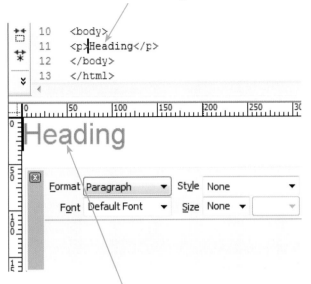

Don't forget

CSS styles can be created for formatting specific elements within a page (such as applying formatting to a piece of text). These are known as class styles. The formatting for entire tags, such as the <p> tag, can also be specified with style sheets.

7 The formatting is visible in Design view as the element is taking the format from the style sheet

8 If a specific style has been created this is included in the code

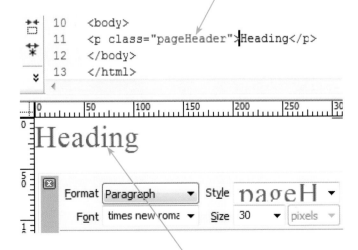

9 The style is applied to the selected item

79

Elements of CSS

When working with CSS there are certain elements within Dreamweaver that are important for creating and editing style sheets. To access these:

80

1 Open the CSS Styles panel by selecting Window, CSS Styles from the menu bar or clicking on the CSS button on the Properties Inspector

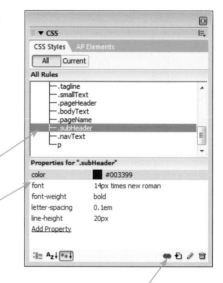

Style-sheet rules are displayed here

Rule properties are displayed here

2 Click on the link button (left-hand button) to attach existing style sheets, or click on the add button (right-hand button) to start creating new style sheets

3 In the New CSS Rule dialog box, click here to create a class rule. This is a uniquely named style that can be applied to specific items in an HTML document

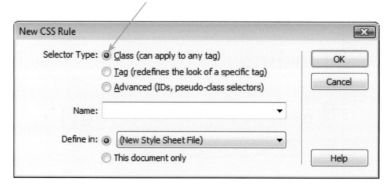

4 Click here to create a rule for an existing HTML tag. This creates properties for the tag that are applied within

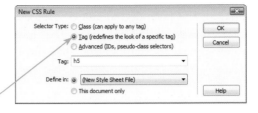

the whole document. For instance, rules can be created for the <body> tag

5 Click here to create a rule for advanced style-sheet features. These are most usually div tags, which can be used to format

content and also to position items with great accuracy

6 Click OK in the New CSS Rule dialog box to access the CSS Rule Definition dialog box. Enter the properties for the CSS rule and click OK to create the rule. This will be available in the CSS Styles panel

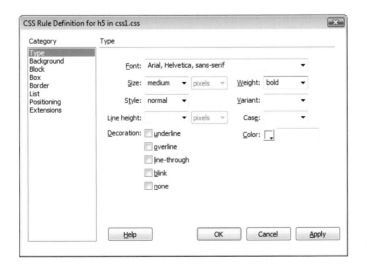

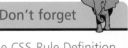

Don't forget

If you create new rules for an existing HTML tag, these rules will apply to all of the affected content in the HTML document. For instance, if the font for the <p> tag is specified as Verdana, any text that appears within this tag will be in Verdana.

Don't forget

The CSS Rule Definition dialog box only contains some of the elements that can be used in style sheets. For a full list of styles, access the O'Reilly CSS Reference panel (Window, Reference from the menu bar) and view the styles in the Styles drop-down box.

CSS layouts

When creating pages with a CSS layout, there are a number of predesigned layouts that can be used as the foundation for the pages. These are HTML pages that have had the relevant CSS rules applied to them so that they display certain formatting. These layouts contain columns that are created in different ways. These are:

● Fixed. This creates columns at a specific size, in pixels

● Elastic. This creates columns that change size if the text size is increased in the browser in which they are being viewed. They do not change size if the browser window is resized

● Liquid. This creates columns that change size if the browser window in which they are being viewed is changed in size

● Hybrid. This creates columns in a combination of the first three options

To create a page with a CSS layout:

1   Select File, New from the menu bar

2   Select the Blank Page option and HTML as the Page Type

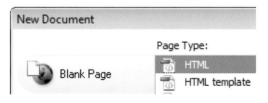

3   Select a CSS layout

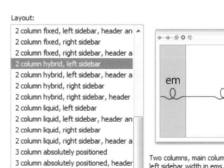

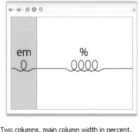

Two columns, main column width in percent, left sidebar width in ems.

4 Click on Create

Create

5 The page is created with the CSS layout and draft content to show the formatting of the page

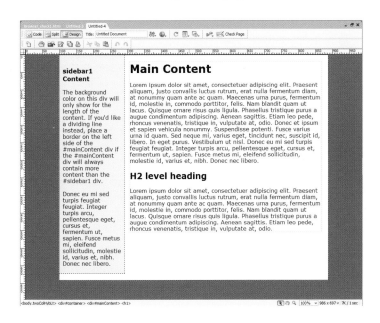

Hot tip

Instead of having the CSS formatting inserted in the head of the HTML file, it is also possible to create a new CSS file for it, or link to an existing CSS file to use additional formatting. This can be done in the New Document window (steps 2 and 3 on the previous page).

6 By default, the CSS formatting is inserted in the head part of the HTML file

```
body  {
    font: 100% Verdana, Arial, Helvetica, sans-serif;
    background: #666666;
    margin: 0; /* it's good practice to zero the margin and padding of the b
*/
    padding: 0;
    text-align: center; /* this centers the container in IE 5* browsers. The
#container selector */
    color: #000000;
}
.twoColHybLt #container {
    width: 80%;  /* this will create a container 80% of the browser width */
    background: #FFFFFF;
    margin: 0 auto; /* the auto margins (in conjunction with a width) center
    border: 1px solid #000000;
    text-align: left; /* this overrides the text-align: center on the body e
}
```

Including style sheets

There are two ways in which style-sheet formatting can be included within an HTML document. One is to include the style-sheet elements within the HTML document itself, and the other is to create an external style sheet and link this to the HTML document. This can be specified when an element for a style sheet is being created:

Don't forget

The <head> section of an HTML document is the one that contains information about the document that is not usually displayed when viewed in a browser. It comes before the <body> section and can contain information such as metadata (for search engines), document type and title and any embedded CSS code.

Hot tip

In general, it is better practice to link to style sheets in a separate file, rather than including the CSS code within an HTML file. This is because it reduces the size of the HTML file and also because it makes it easier to update a lot of linked files, as the changes only have to be made in the single CSS file rather than in every individual HTML file.

1 Click here to create a new style sheet in an external file and link it to the document

2 Click here to include the style-sheet elements within the head section of the current document

3 If the style-sheet elements are included within the current document the code is included here

```
<title>Restaurant - Home Page</title>
<meta http-equiv="Content-Type" content="text/html; charset=utf-8" />
<style type="text/css">
<!--
.heading_text {
    font-family: Verdana, Arial, Helvetica, sans-serif;
    font-size: x-large;
    font-style: normal;
    color: #990000;
}
-->
</style>
</head>
```

4 If a style sheet is attached as an external file the reference to the file is included here in the code

```
<head>
<title>Restaurant - Home Page</title>
<meta http-equiv="Content-Type" content="text/html; charset=utf-8" />

<link href="css1.css" rel="stylesheet" type="text/css" />

</head>
```

Cascading style sheets

As the name suggests, styles can be cascaded within a document. This means that one style can be applied to an item, such as a block of text, and then other styles can be applied within the first style. This gives a lot of flexibility for creating complex formatting effects, although some CSS elements will overrule others. To apply cascading styles:

Beware

When applying styles to text, highlight the individual words rather than clicking within the text block. If words are highlighted they will have the style applied just to them; if the cursor is inserted in the text block, the style will apply to the whole block.

1 Apply a style to an element within a document. In this case it is a piece of text. The style is included within the code

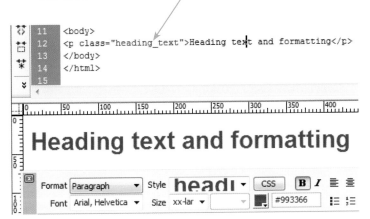

Don't forget

2 Select another item within the text and add another style to it. Within the code, the second style is inserted inside the first one

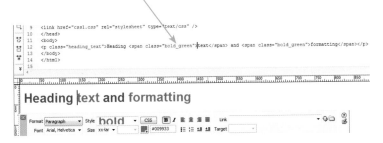

In the code, "span" indicates that a class style has been applied to a specifically selected element, rather than a whole block of content. For instance, if a word of text within a paragraph has "span" before it in the code this means that a class style has been applied to this item and not the rest of the paragraph. To apply a style to a whole paragraph, insert the cursor in the paragraph and then select the required class style from the Properties Inspector.

CSS Styles panel

The CSS Styles panel is a vital item when creating and editing style sheets. All of the rules and properties of associated style sheets are displayed within the CSS Styles panel and elements can be added and edited here too. If the CSS Styles panel is not visible, select Window, CSS Styles from the menu bar, or click the CSS button on the Properties Inspector to open the CSS Styles panel. To use the CSS Styles panel:

1 Click here to display all of the available style sheets for a document and their properties

2 Click here to display the rules of a selected style sheet

3 Click here to select a specific rule within the style sheet

4 Click here to edit one of the properties of the selected rule

5 The changes are made in the CSS Styles panel, and they will also take effect within the style sheet and any linked documents

6 Click here to view the style-sheet details of the currently selected item within the document

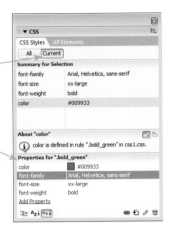

7 The properties of the currently selected item are displayed here

8 Click here to display the properties of a selected item and all of the other available CSS properties

9 Click here to display the property families. Click on a plus sign to see the available properties for each family

CSS management

If you work with CSS frequently, there will be times when you want to use a certain piece of CSS in more than one document. It would be feasible to copy and paste the relevant CSS text, but Dreamweaver provides the means to manage all of your CSS code, through the CSS panel. To do this:

1   Click a rule in the CSS panel

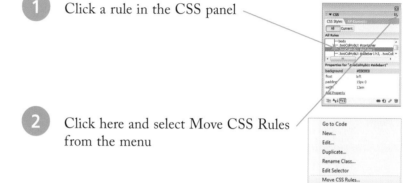

Don't forget

It is generally best practice to include CSS in a linked file, rather than embed it in the head part of a single page.

2   Click here and select Move CSS Rules from the menu

3   Click on the "Style sheet" button and then the Browse button to select an existing style sheet

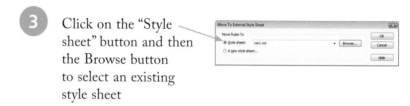

4   Click on the "A new style sheet" button and click OK

5   Create a new style sheet within your website structure. The new rule will be included in the new file

Browser Compatibility Check

As there are now an increasing number of browsers on the market it is important to check how CSS content will perform on each of the different platforms (because of its complexity, CSS code can be rendered differently on different browsers). Within Dreamweaver there is a facility to check the compatibility of CSS in different browsers. To do this:

1 Click on the Check Page button on the Document toolbar and select Check Browser Compatibility

Don't forget

All CSS code in the CSS layouts is compatible with the different browsers covered by the Browser Compatibility Check function.

2 Any compatibility issues are displayed here

3 If there are no compatibility issues, this is noted at the bottom-left of the window

No issues detected.

4 Click on this button to change the settings for the browsers to be checked

5 Specify the versions of different browsers to be checked and click OK

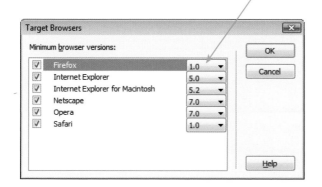

CSS Advisor

CSS can be a complicated, and constantly developing, subject if you want to start writing and using your own rules. However, help is at hand in the form of an online CSS forum called the CSS Advisor. This has discussions about the latest CSS issues and uses and it is somewhere to swap ideas and experiences with like-minded CSS users. To access the CSS Advisor:

1 Access the Browser Compatibility Check window as shown on the previous page

2 Click on the Check Adobe.com link to access the CSS Advisor site

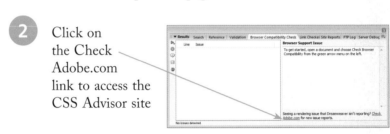

Seeing a rendering issue that Dreamweaver isn't reporting? Check Adobe.com for new issue reports.

3 Click on one of the subjects to view all of the relevant posts and comments. It is also possible to submit your own posts about a CSS topic

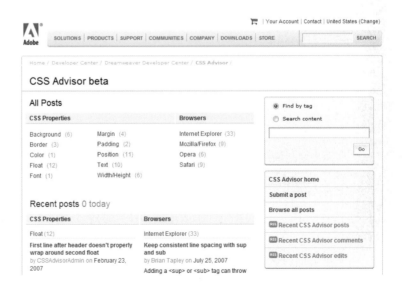

6 Formatting with CSS

This chapter shows how to format content in HTML files, through the use of CSS. It covers creating and editing style sheets and also details the different types of CSS rules that can be created and applied. The concept of positioning items with CSS is also covered.

Attaching a style sheet

One of the quickest ways of adding CSS to a web page is to attach a style sheet to an existing HTML document. This can be done with a style sheet that you have created yourself, or there are sample ones contained within Dreamweaver that can be used. To do this:

Don't forget

Using sample style sheets is a quick way to see how an attached style sheet affects the formatting and look of an HTML file.

1 Open the CSS Styles panel and click here to attach an external style sheet

2 Click here to access the sample style sheets

3 Select a style sheet from the samples and click OK

4 Details of the attached style sheet are displayed in the CSS Styles panel. Click here to show and hide all of the rules within the style sheet

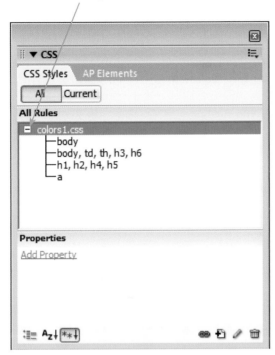

5 When content is added to the page it takes on the appropriate style from the style sheet. For instance, when body content is added, it takes on the properties of the "body" rule in the style sheet. Similarly, if styles such as "h1" are applied, these take on the properties of the corresponding rule in the style sheet

Creating a style sheet

In addition to using sample style sheets it is also possible to create your own style sheets for a document. This can be done by manually writing the CSS code, but an easier way is to create it by using the CSS Styles panel. To do this:

1 Open the CSS Styles panel and click here

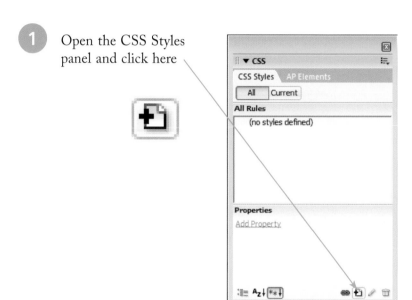

2 Select an option for creating a new rule within a style sheet

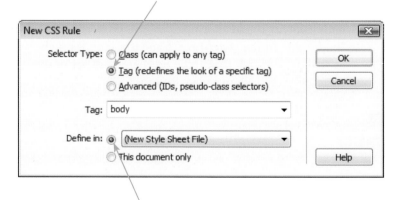

3 Select this button to create a new external style sheet and click OK

4 Select a name and location for the new style sheet and click Save

Don't forget

Save a new style sheet in the same site folder as the file to which it is linked, or create a new CSS folder and save your style sheets here.

5 Enter the properties for the rule selected in step 2 and click OK

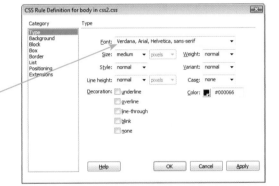

95

Hot tip

Click the Apply button to see style changes as they are made, without leaving the CSS Rule Definition window.

6 Details of the newly created style sheet are displayed in the CSS Styles panel. The properties for the rule created in step 5 are displayed here

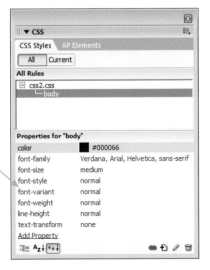

Editing style sheets

The CSS Styles panel provides great flexibility for editing style sheets once they have been created and attached to a document:

Beware

Coding for CSS files is a lot stricter than for HTML files: if one element of the code syntax is missing or entered in the wrong place then that part of the code will not function.

1 Open the CSS Styles panel and select a style sheet or a rule within it

2 Click here to edit the style-sheet file

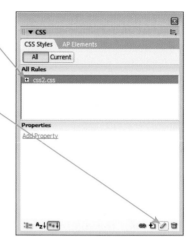

3 The style sheet is opened as a separate document (denoted by a .css extension). Elements of the style sheet can then be edited directly within the code of the style sheet

Don't forget

Changes made directly within a CSS file have to be saved before they take effect.

Editing with the CSS Styles panel

Elements can also be edited using the CSS Styles panel:

1 Select a rule within an attached style sheet. The rule's properties are displayed here

2 Select a property within the style and click here to edit the rules of the property

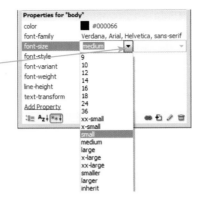

3 The new attributes for the property are displayed within the CSS Styles panel. This will also have been updated in the style-sheet file

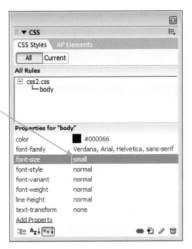

Hot tip

If a CSS rule or property is edited in the CSS Styles panel the relevant CSS file will be opened and updated automatically at the same time.

4 Click the Add Property link to add a new property to the rule and enter the attributes for the property

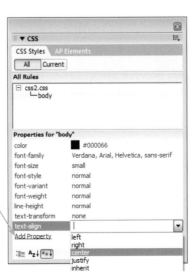

Adding new CSS rules

In addition to using the CSS Styles panel to edit the existing rules of a style sheet, you can also use it to add new rules to an existing style sheet. To do this:

1 Open the CSS Styles panel and select an existing style sheet or a rule within it

2 Click here to add a new rule

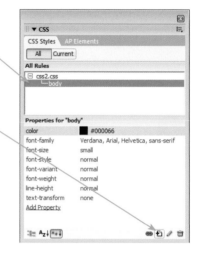

3 Select the type of rule to be created. Make sure the rule is to be defined in an existing style sheet. Click OK

4 Enter the properties for the rule and click OK

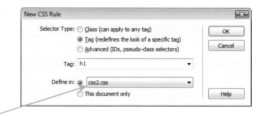

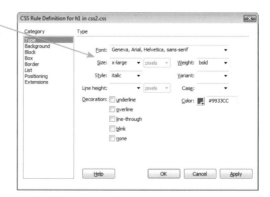

...cont'd

5 The new rule is added here within the CSS Styles panel

6 The properties for the new rule are displayed here within the panel

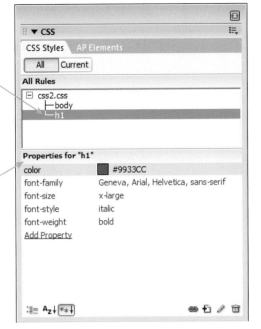

Beware

When a new rule is added to a style sheet via the CSS Styles panel, the style-sheet file is opened and updated automatically. This then has to be saved to retain the new rule.

99

7 The new rule and its properties are also added to the CSS file

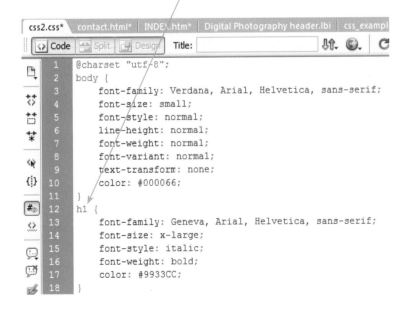

Creating class styles

Class styles within a style sheet are rules that are created with unique names that can then be applied to certain elements of a web page. This can be particularly useful for adding specific formatting to individual elements within a page. For instance, you may want to use red text for emphasis, and this can be achieved by creating an appropriate class style. To create class styles:

100

Apparently you can name the tag anything, as long as it's proceeded by a . dot.

Ex •speaker
(speaker of a block quote)

1 Open the CSS Styles panel and click here to create a new rule

2 Click here to create a new class rule

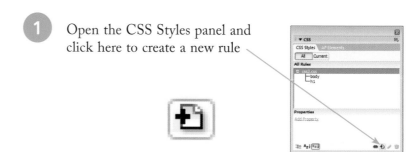

3 Enter a unique name for the rule and click OK

4 Enter the properties for the class rule

5 Click OK

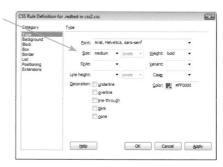

6 The class rule and its properties are added to the CSS Styles panel

Applying styles

Once class styles have been created they can then be applied to elements within the web page. This can be done with any element including text, images and tables. To apply class styles:

1 Select a piece of content on a page. For text, this can either be done by clicking within a text block (which applies the style to the whole block) or by highlighting specific text (which applies the style to the highlighted section)

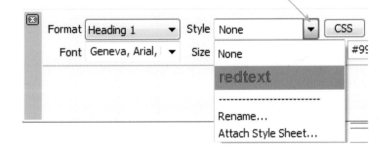

Hot tip

Styles can also be added directly from the CSS Styles panel. To do this, highlight an item and right-click (Windows) or Ctrl+click (Mac) on a style in the CSS Styles panel. Select Apply, to apply the style to the selected item.

2 Click here in the Properties Inspector and select a class style

3 The style is applied to the selected item on the page

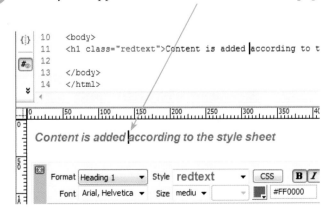

101

Creating div tags

One way in which CSS styles can be used to format and position elements on a web page is through the use of div tags. These act as containers for content and they are particularly useful for positioning items on a page, independently from other elements. To create div tags:

1 Open the CSS Styles panel and click here to create a new CSS rule

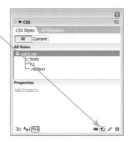

2 Click here to create a div tag

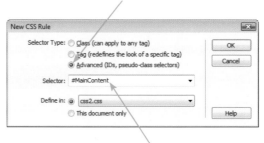

3 Enter the name for the div tag and click OK

4 Enter the properties for the div tag. Click here to set the positioning of the div tag. This can be used to specify exactly where it will appear on the page. Click OK to create the div tag

Inserting div tags

Div tags can be included on a page and then have the content added to them, or an item can be selected and then have the div tag applied to it. Either way the process for inserting the div tag is the same:

1 Click on the Layout tab of the Insert panel and click here, or select Insert, Layout Objects, Div Tag from the menu bar

2 Click here and select the name of a div tag that has been created. Click OK

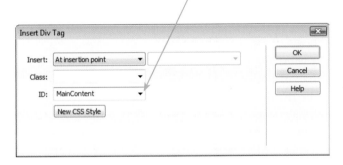

3 The div tag is added to the page and content can then be added within it. Check the code to see how the div tag is entered

Beware

Each div tag can only be used once in each file. If you have one div tag and it has already been used, the ID box in the Insert Div Tag dialog box will be empty: i.e. there will be nothing to select.

103

Don't forget

Div tags can be edited from within the CSS Styles panel in the same way as any other CSS elements in the panel.

Positioning with CSS

One of the great advantages of CSS is the ability to position items with great accuracy. This can be done with most CSS elements, but the best way to do it is to create a div tag for a particular item and then apply the positioning to the div tag itself. Any items within the div tag will then be positioned accordingly. To position items with div tags:

1 Create a div tag and click OK to add the rule definitions for the tag

2 Click the Box category in the CSS Rule Definition dialog box and enter a value for the size of the box for the div tag. This creates a container at a specific size for any content that is added

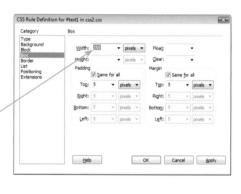

3 Click the Positioning category and select "absolute" for the type of positioning. This will place the div tag in exactly the position specified in this dialog box: i.e. it will not move around the page

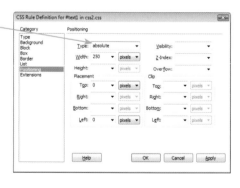

4 Set the position for where the box will be placed (this is measured from the top-left of the page)

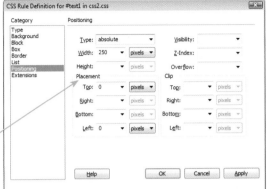

5 Click OK

6 The div tag is entered into the code of the file and the tagged content is displayed on the page, according to the properties specified in the CSS Rule Definition dialog box

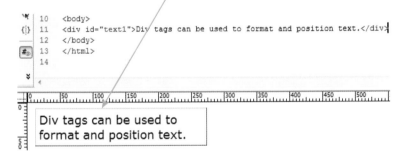

7 Other div tags can also be used to position different blocks of content with great precision

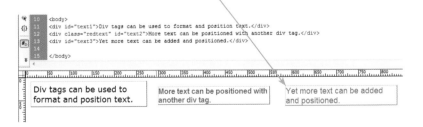

Beware

Once an item has been positioned with a div tag, preview the page in your default browser to make sure it appears as expected.

105

Don't forget

Empty div tags can be inserted into a file and then have content added to them. Alternatively, content can be selected and then have the div tag applied to it. Either way, the content will be positioned and formatted according to the properties of the inserted div tag.

Floating items

Another way to position items on a page is to use the "float" option. This can be used to position items to the left or right of the page, so that other elements can then wrap around them in that position. The float option can be used on any CSS rule, but probably the best way is to use it within a div tag. To do this:

1 Add an element that you want to float left or right of the page

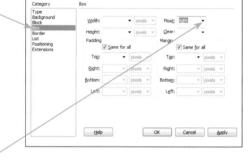

2 Create a div tag and select the Box category in the CSS Rule Definition dialog box

3 Click here and select "left" or "right" for the float property

4 Click OK

5 Apply the div tag to the element by selecting it and selecting Insert, Layout Options, Div Tag from the menu bar

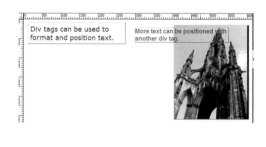

6 The element is positioned accordingly

Other CSS properties

The other categories of properties that can be applied through the CSS Rule Definition dialog box are:

1. Background. This contains properties for the background of a rule. These include background color, background image, and how a background element appears and is positioned

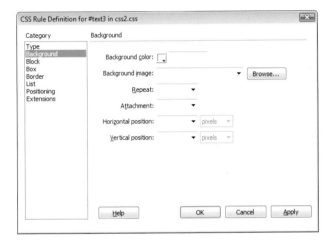

2. Block. Properties in this category relate mainly to text spacing and alignment

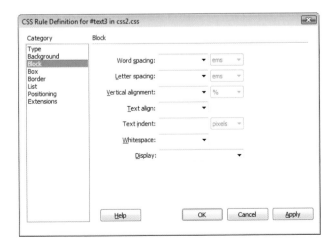

...cont'd

3 Border. This contains properties for the border of an element – for instance, the border of a table. The settings include style, width and the color of the border

4 List. This allows you to change the appearance of lists within a rule. The settings available include type of bullet, image for the bullet and the bullet's position

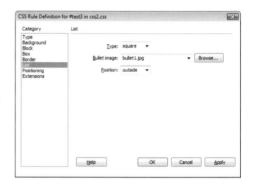

5 Extensions. This contains properties for elements such as page breaks for printing, the appearance of the cursor and special effects

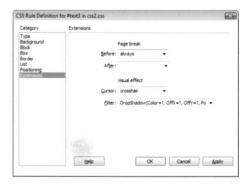

7 Using hyperlinks

This chapter looks at how items on web pages can be linked together through the use of hyperlinks. It also shows how to create image maps and navigation bars.

About hyperlinks

Without hyperlinks (or just links), the Web would be an unconnected collection of pages and sites that would be tortuous to navigate around since you would have to specify the Web address (URL) for each page that you wanted to view. Hyperlinks simplify this process considerably: they are pieces of HTML coding that create "clickable" regions on a web page – users can click on a hyperlink and it will take them to the linked item. In simple terms, hyperlinks are shortcuts for jumping between elements on the Web.

Both text and images can be used as hyperlinks: text usually appears underlined when it is acting as a hyperlink and, for both elements, the cursor turns into a pointing hand when it is positioned over a hyperlink on a web page.

The code for a simple hyperlink to a page within the same site structure could look like this:

<a href="news.htm">Latest News</a>

In this example the words "Latest News" would be underlined on the page, and when the user clicks on them, the page "news.htm" will open.

Types of hyperlinks

There are different types of hyperlinks depending on what they are linking to:

- Absolute links. These are links that go externally to other pages on the Web. This means that the full URL has to be inserted so that the browser knows where to look, e.g. http://www.ineasysteps.com/

- Relative links. These are links to files within the same site structure. Such a link would appear in the following format:
  <a href="main.htm">My Day</a>

- Email links. These are links to specific email addresses. These are created with the following code as the link:
  <a href="mailto:nickvandome@hotmail.com">Nick Vandome</a>

Don't forget

URL stands for Uniform Resource Locator and it refers to the unique address of every page on the Web.

Don't forget

Some of the items hyperlinks can be linked to include other pages within the same website, other locations on the same page, other websites and email addresses.

Don't forget

For relative links, the notation "../" in a hyperlink address means move up one level in the folder hierarchy, and "/" means move down one level in the hierarchy.

Linking to documents

Links can be created to a variety of documents, including images, sounds and video clips, but the most common type of link is to another web page. Dreamweaver provides a number of ways to achieve this:

Using the Properties Inspector

1 Select an image or piece of text that you want to make into a link

2 Click here and enter the URL of the page to which you want to link

or

Click here to browse your hard drive for a file to link to. Once you have chosen one, click on OK (Windows) or Choose (Mac)

3 The selected file will now be visible here in the Properties Inspector

Beware

If you are using images as hyperlinks, make sure that they are clearly identifiable, otherwise the user may think they are just a graphical design feature.

Beware

If you browse to a file outside your current site structure, and try and link to it, a warning box will appear alerting you to the fact that the file is not contained within the current structure. You will be given the option of then saving it within the current structure. This will ensure that the link is correct.

...cont'd

Using the Menu bar

1 Select an image or piece of text that you want to make into a link

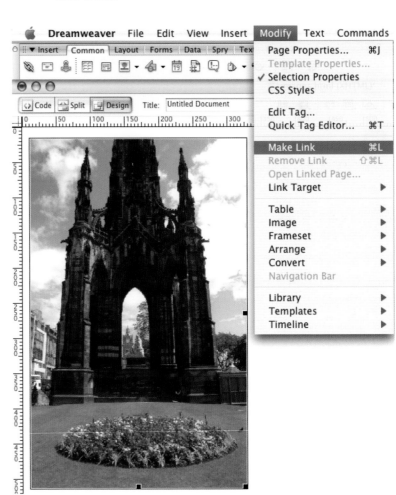

Don't forget

Hyperlinks can be edited or removed by selecting the link, clicking on Modify, Change Link (or Remove Link) from the menu bar and selecting a new file from your hard drive. Alternatively, right-click (Windows) or Ctrl+click (Mac) on a link and select Change Link (or Remove Link) from the contextual menu.

2 Select Modify, Make Link from the menu bar and select a file as shown on the previous page

Linking to anchors

As well as creating hyperlinks to other pages within your own site, and external sites, it is also possible to use links to move about the same page. This can be particularly useful if you have a lot of text on a page, or several sections, and you want to enable the users to navigate around the page without having to scroll down it too much. In Dreamweaver this is done through the use of anchors. These are inserted on the page at the required points and hyperlinks are then created to them from other parts of the page. To do this:

1 Insert the cursor at the point where you want the anchor to appear

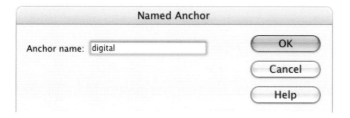

2 Select Insert, Named Anchor from the menu bar

3 In the Named Anchor dialog box, type a name for the anchor. This is the name that will be used in the link. Click OK

4 The anchor will be denoted on the page by this element. Click on it to see the anchor's properties

Don't forget

Anchors are also known as bookmarks in other web authoring programs. In Dreamweaver they are invisible elements, which means they are not seen on the published page.

Hot tip

It is not necessary to select an image or a piece of text when creating an anchor. The anchor is independent of any other item on the page and is placed at the insertion point.

Beware

When naming anchors, give them a single-word name. It is possible to enter more than one word in the dialog box, but this can cause problems when the link is trying to find the anchor name.

...cont'd

5 Select the image or piece of text on the page that is going to act as the link to the named anchor

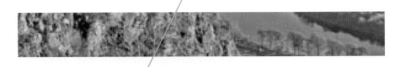
Hot tip

If you are using a lot of anchors on a page, it is advisable to include links back to the top of the page. This means that the user will not feel lost in the middle of a long document. To include a link back to the beginning of a document, insert an anchor at the top of the page and name it "Top". Then move further down the document and type "Top" or "Top of Page". Select the text and create a hyperlink to "#Top". When clicked, this should then take the user to the "Top" anchor at the beginning of the document.

6 In the Properties Inspector, enter the name of the anchor in the Link box, preceded by the "#" symbol

Link | #digital |

Target

7 It is also possible to link to an anchor in another document, in which case the full filename should be inserted in the Link box, followed by the "#" symbol and the anchor name as above

Link | vw.nickvandome.com#digital

Target

Don't forget

Press F12 or select File, Preview in Browser to test the page in a browser and make sure that the link goes to the correct anchor.

Creating an email link

To create a link that allows the user to access an email address, first insert the cursor at the point where you want the link to appear; then, to create the email link:

1 Click on the Email Link button on the Common tab on the Insert panel

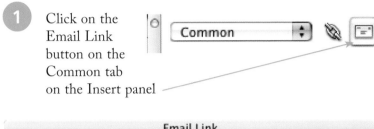

2 In the Email Link dialog box, insert the text that will be displayed for the link and enter the email address to which the link will point. Click OK

3 The linked text will appear on the page and when it is selected

the email address to which it is linked will be shown in the Properties Inspector. When the link is activated in a browser, the user's email program will open, with the address pre-inserted in the To box

Point-to-File links

When you are creating links, there may be times when you do not want to insert the filename of the document to which you want to link, but rather just point to a file and instruct Dreamweaver to link to that item. With the Point-to-File tool you can do just that. Dreamweaver even lets you use it in several different ways.

Point-to-File in the document window

The Point-to-File tool can be used to link two files that have both been opened in the document window:

Beware

The Point-to-File technique cannot be used to create links to external web pages, even if they are opened next to the document window.

1 Resize the two open files so that they are both visible in the document window

2 Select the item that you want to use as the link

Don't forget

To position two files next to each other select Window, Tile Horizontally (or Vertically) from the menu bar.

3 Select this icon in the Properties Inspector and drag it into the file to be linked to

Point-to-File in the site window

1 Select Site, Site Map from the menu bar

2 Select a file in the Site Map window

Don't forget

The Point-to-File technique can also be used to link to an anchor point that has been inserted into a page.

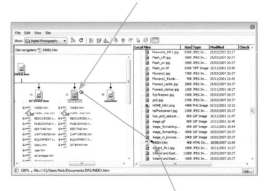

3 Click on this icon and drag to one of the files in the Local Files list

Image maps

An image map is a device that allows you to insert links to multiple files within a single image. Links within an image map are created with "hotspots" which are drawn over an image. Image maps can be used with any image that has easily identifiable areas. To create an image map:

1 Insert the image that is going to serve as the image map and select it by clicking on it once

2 In the Properties Inspector, click on one of the Hotspot tools

3 Draw an area on the image that is going to act as a hotspot. This is the area that the user will be able to click on and jump to the linked file

4 After a hotspot has been drawn, enter a file to link to here, or browse to select a file from your hard drive

Don't forget

Dreamweaver uses client-side image maps, which means the linked information is stored within the HTML document itself. The other type of image map is a server-side one, which contains the linking information in a separate file. In general, client-side image maps operate more quickly.

Beware

Do not overlap hotspots, or the user may have problems linking to the correct file.

Don't forget

Click on the arrow next to the Hotspot tool, if you want to select a hotspot. This can be used to select hotspots, move them or resize them. If you want to change a link for a hotspot you first have to select it with this tool.

Navigation bars

One of the best devices for moving around a website is a navigation bar. This is a set of buttons that contain links to the other main areas of the site. Once a navigation bar has been created, it can be stored and placed on as many pages as required.

When a navigation bar is created, each button can have a different image assigned to it depending on its state, i.e. how it is interacting with the cursor (see the margin note). To create a navigation bar:

Hot tip

Each button on a navigation bar can have four different states, having separate images: "Up" is the state when the button is inactive; "Over" is the state when the cursor is passed over the button; "Down" is the state when the button is pressed; "Over while down" is the state after the button has been released.

1 Create the images that you want to use for the various states of the buttons in the navigation bar and click on the Navigation Bar button on the Common tab on the Insert panel

2 Name the first element of the navigation bar

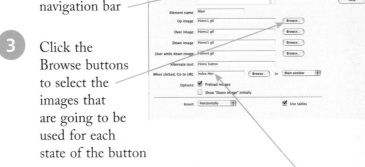

3 Click the Browse buttons to select the images that are going to be used for each state of the button

4 Click here to enter the page to which the button will link

5 Click to add each button to the navigation bar. Repeat steps 2–4 for each button you want to include

6 Click OK

Beware

Each individual page can only have one navigation bar on it. In general, it is best to use the same navigation bar for a complete site.

8 Using tables

This chapter shows how tables can be used to format the content of web pages. It explains how to create tables, edit and format them and also how to add content.

Designing with tables

One of the biggest challenges for any web designer is to create a page layout that is both versatile and visually appealing. This invariably involves combining text and images and, before the advent of tables in HTML, it was a considerable problem trying to get everything in the right place. Even when elements looked correct on the designer's computer, there was no guarantee that they would appear the same when viewed on different computers and with different browsers. However, tables changed all that.

HTML tables are one of the most important design tools that are available to web authors. Although their name suggests that they should perhaps only be used to collate and display figures, this is definitely not the case: tables can contain the same content as is placed at any other point on an HTML page. They can then be used to position different elements and, since each item can be placed in its own individual cell within the table, the designer can be confident that this is the position in which they will appear, regardless of the browser used.

Tables can be used for simple formatting techniques, such as aligning text and images, or they can be used to create complex page designs:

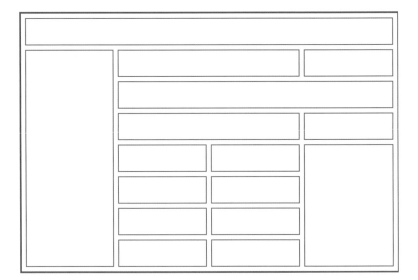

120

Inserting a table

You can insert as many tables as you like on a page, and tables can also be nested, i.e. tables placed within other tables. This provides even more versatility in the design process. When a table is inserted, various attributes can be set initially. However, it is also possible to edit and amend a table's attributes at any time after it has been created. To insert a table:

1 On the Common tab on the Insert panel, click on the Table button

2 Enter the number of rows and columns that are required for the table

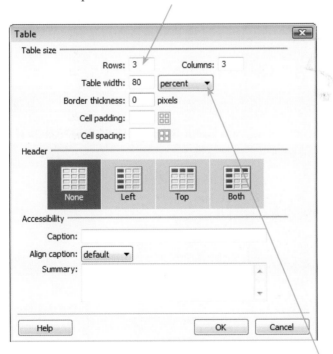

3 Enter a value for the size of the table. Click here to select a percentage or a pixel size. If it is a percentage, this will be a percentage of the browser window in which it is being viewed. The pixel size is the actual physical size of the table

Don't forget

Tables can also be created by selecting Insert, Table from the menu bar. This brings up the same dialog box as using the Insert panel.

Hot tip

Use the percentage setting for the width of a table if you want to make sure it will all fit in the user's browser. However this could affect the way some of the content is displayed within the table. Use the pixel setting if you want the formatting to remain exactly as designed.

...cont'd

4 Enter a size for the table border. A value of 0 will create an invisible border and the default value is 1

5 Enter values for the cell padding and the cell spacing. Cell padding affects how much space there is around each item in a cell and cell spacing affects how much space there is between the cells in a table

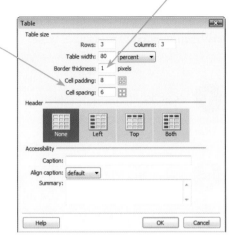

Don't forget

If the cell padding is increased, the size of the individual cells increases too, since the area for adding content in the cell is still the same, it is just the area around it that increases. If the cell spacing is increased, the size of the cells decreases, to accommodate the space around them.

6 Click OK to create the table

A table with cell padding and cell spacing both at 1

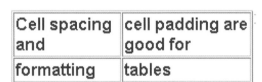

Cell spacing and	cell padding are good for
formatting	tables

A table with cell padding and cell spacing both at 10

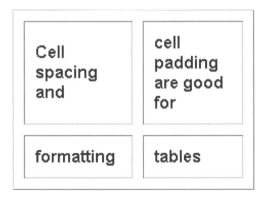

Cell spacing and	cell padding are good for
formatting	tables

Adding a table header

When creating a table it can be useful to insert a header describing its contents. This is particularly important from an accessibility point of view, i.e. for people who are blind or partially sighted and will be accessing the website through a device that will read the content on the page. To add a descriptive header:

1 Select one of the Header options

2 Enter a description for the header

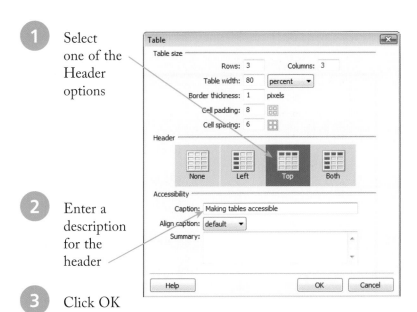

3 Click OK

4 The header is displayed in a separate row in the table

Don't forget

The header does not affect any of the other properties of the table – it will still have the same number of columns and rows.

123

Making tables accessible

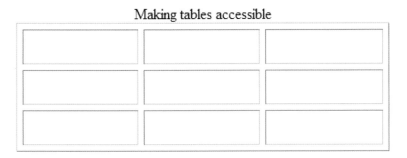

Editing a table

If you create a table and then decide you want to change some of its attributes, it is possible to do so through the Properties Inspector. In addition to the settings that can be used in the Insert Table dialog box, there are also some other attributes that can be used:

1 Click once on a table's border, to select it. A thick black line with three resizing handles should appear around it

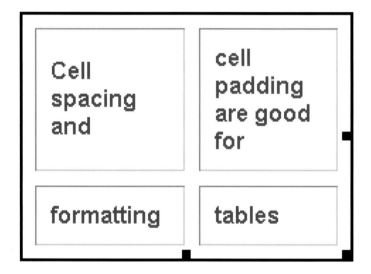

2 Once a table is selected the Table Properties Inspector will appear:

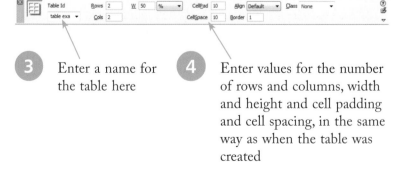

3 Enter a name for the table here

4 Enter values for the number of rows and columns, width and height and cell padding and cell spacing, in the same way as when the table was created

5 Click here to access options for aligning the table on the page: this can be Left, Center or Right

6 Click here to access additional table properties – see below

7 Clear cell height or width

8 Change the table height or width to pixels or percent

9 Click here to select a background color for the table (left box) and an outer border color (right box)

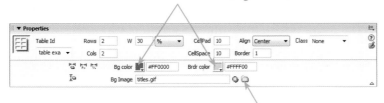

10 Click here to select an image for the table background

Rows and columns

When tables are being used, particularly for complex designs, it is unlikely that the correct number of rows and columns will be specified first time. As shown on page 124, it is possible to increase or decrease the number of rows and columns by selecting the table and amending the values in the Table Properties Inspector. This can also be achieved as follows:

1 Insert the cursor in the table where you want to add or delete rows or columns. Right-click (Windows) or Ctrl+click (Mac) and select Table

2 Insert a single row or column by selecting Insert Row or Insert Column

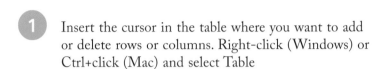

3 To insert multiple rows or columns, click Insert Rows or Columns

4 In the dialog box, enter whether you want to insert rows or columns, the number to be inserted and where you want them placed in relation to the insertion point

5 Click OK to insert the specified number of rows or columns

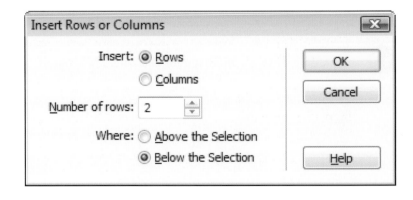

Selecting cells

Once a table has been created it can be useful to select individual cells, or groups of cells, so that specific formatting options can be applied to them. For instance, you may want to have a table where the top row of cells is a different size or color from the rest of the cells in the table. Or you may want to apply separate formatting options to single cells.

Selecting cells

Insert the cursor in the cell you want to select; hold and drag to the outer border of the cell. A thick dark line appears around the cell to indicate that it has been selected. To select more than one cell, keep dragging until all of the required cells have been covered

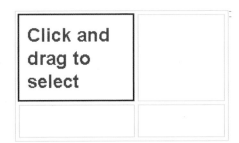

Merging cells

Once cells have been selected, it is then possible to merge them together, independently of the other cells in the table. This is an excellent formatting device as it allows the designer to break the symmetrical pattern of a table, which gives increased flexibility. To merge cells once they have been selected:

1 With the required cells selected, right-click (Windows) or Ctrl+click (Mac) and select Table, Merge Cells

2 Or click here on the Properties Inspector

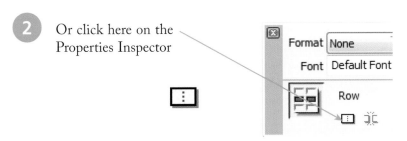

127

Hot tip

If the cell you are trying to select is in the first column of a table, you have to drag the cursor to the right-hand border of the cell. If it is in the last column of a table, you have to drag the cursor to the left-hand border of the cell. If the cell you are trying to select is in any other column in the table, it can be selected by dragging the cursor to the left- or right-hand border. Similarly for selecting a cell within rows in a table.

Hot tip

Entire rows and columns can be selected by positioning the cursor on a border until a thick black arrow appears and clicking once.

Don't forget

Cells can also be merged by selecting them and then selecting Modify, Table, Merge Cells from the menu bar.

...cont'd

3 The selected cells are now merged, independently of the other cells in the table

Splitting cells

Any cell within a table can be split into smaller parts, regardless of whether it has already been merged or not. To do this:

Beware

The Split Cell option is only available if you select a single cell. If you try and activate this command when more than one cell is selected it will be grayed out, i.e. unavailable.

1 Insert the cursor in the cell you want to split

2 Right-click (Windows) or Ctrl+click (Mac) and select Table, Split Cell from the contextual menu

3 Or click here on the Properties Inspector

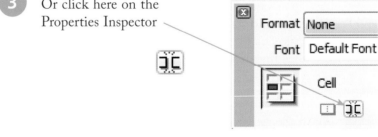

Don't forget

If you split a cell that contains content, i.e. text or images, this will be placed in the left-hand cell if the cell is split by columns, and the top cell if it is split by rows.

4 In the Split Cell dialog box, select whether you want to split the cell into rows or columns, and the required number. Click OK

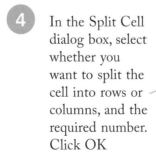

Adding content

If an item can be added to a page within Dreamweaver, then it can be inserted in a table too. A table acts only as a placeholder for content; it does not determine the type of content that can be displayed.

Adding text

1 Insert the cursor in the cell in which you want to include the text

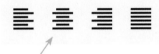

2 Enter the text and click on one of these buttons in the Properties Inspector to align it

Adding images and more

Images, and most forms of multimedia content, can also be added to a table:

1 Insert the cursor in the cell in which you want to insert the image or other content

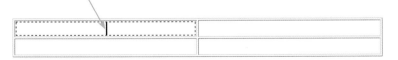

2 Click on the Image button on the Common tab on the Insert panel and select an item from your hard drive

129

Hot tip

If you are including text and images in the same cell, insert a paragraph break <p> </p> between them. This will make it possible to align them independently of each other.

Hot tip

If you are including text and images in the same cell, make sure the No Wrap option is not checked. Otherwise the text will continue to fill the cell, and keep expanding it, rather than moving down onto the next line.

Beware

If an image is larger than the cell it is being inserted into, the cell will automatically expand to accommodate the item. This could have the effect of distorting the size of the rest of the cells in the table.

Expanded view

Expanded view is a feature that makes it easier to select parts of a table and also elements within it. When working in Expanded view, additional cell padding and spacing is added to the table, but this is just a visual aid and will not affect the appearance of the table when viewed in a web browser. To access Expanded view and select elements within a table:

1 Select the Layout tab on the Insert panel

2 Click on the Expanded button

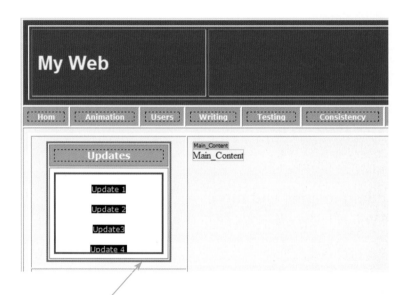

3 Click on the expanded borders to select the table or select items within the cells

4 Click here to return to Standard view

9 Spry elements

This chapter looks at dynamic elements that can be added to web pages.

Spry overview

Any user of the Web knows that there are a lot of impressive and sophisticated effects that can be included within web pages. A lot of these effects require complicated coding that is too daunting for many designers. However, in Dreamweaver CS3 there is a set of tools that can create these types of effects using a graphical interface. This is known as the Spry Framework.

The Spry Framework is a library of items created in Javascript code that can be inserted into pages within Dreamweaver to create effects such as sophisticated menu bars, tabbed panels and text-validation fields.

There are several Spry elements that can be used, but the process is similar for all of them:

Don't forget

The full name for the Spry elements in Dreamweaver is Spry Framework for Ajax.

1 Click on the Spry tab on the Insert panel and select one of the elements

2 The selected item is added to the Dreamweaver page

Don't forget

Completed Spry elements are a combination of HTML, CSS and Javascript code.

3 Each Spry effect has CSS style sheets attached to it and these are automatically added to the CSS Styles panel

④ A SpryAssets folder is created, containing all of the code that is required for the Spry item

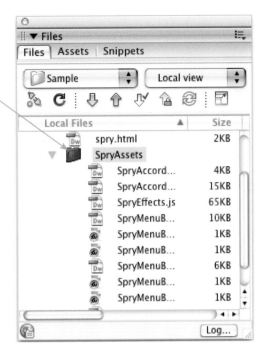

Don't forget

The SpryAssets folder is created automatically once a Spry element has been added to a page and the page has been saved.

⑤ When the Spry item is previewed in a browser, its full functionality is displayed

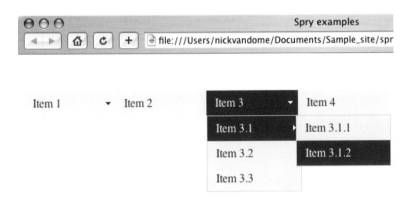

Beware

While Spry elements can be added visually to a Dreamweaver page, the code that is used to create them can be considerably more complicated.

Spry widgets

Spry widgets are a collection of items that can add sophisticated functionality to a web page.

Spry Menu Bar

This widget creates drop-down menus:

1 Click here on the Spry menu

2 Select the orientation for the menu bar and click OK

3 The Menu Bar widget is added to the Dreamweaver page

4 Formatting can be done in the Properties Inspector

5 Preview the Menu Bar in a browser to see its operation

Spry Accordion

This widget creates panels that can be collapsed or expanded according to the content that is required to be viewed:

1 Click here on the Spry menu

2 The Accordion widget is added to the Dreamweaver page

Don't forget

The Spry Accordion widget is a useful option if you want to display one item of information while hiding another.

3 Formatting can be done in the Properties Inspector

4 When the Accordion widget is previewed, click on a heading to view the content for that section

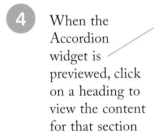

Don't forget

Two of the other Spry widgets are Tabbed Panels and Collapsible Panel. Both of these can be added in a similar way to the items on these pages.

5 Click on another panel to view the content within that one and close the other one

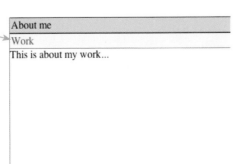

...cont'd

Spry Validation

There is a group of widgets that can be used to validate items on a web page, i.e. ensure that the correct format of text is entered by the user when using items such as forms. This means that if the date has to be entered in a specific format, the user cannot proceed until they have added this correctly. Text validation can also be used, for example, to ensure users enter their name when filling in a form. There are four main Spry Validation items and these are:

● TextField, where text has to be entered in a specific format

● Select, where an item has to be selected from a drop-down menu

● Checkbox, where at least one checkbox in a group has to be selected

● Textarea, where a block of text has to be entered

The process for inserting Spry Validation items is similar for all of them and this example is for a TextField:

Beware

Spry Validation items are created within a form environment. If the Validation item is not completed correctly it will not be possible to send the form.

1 Select one of the Validation widgets on the Spry menu (this is the TextField one)

2 The widget is added to the Dreamweaver page

Spry TextField: sprytextfield1

| | Invalid format. |

3 In the Properties Inspector, select the type for the TextField (e.g. Date) and the format in which the text must be entered

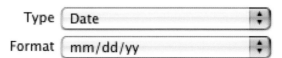

4 Click here to specify the text that appears if text is entered in an incorrect format

5 Click here to select how the validation process is triggered

Preview states [Invalid Format ▲▼]

Validate on ☑ Blur ☐ Change ☑ Submit

Don't forget

The Blur validation trigger is activated once the user has added data and then clicked outside the text box.

6 In the "Init val" box, enter the text that will initially appear in the text box

Init val [Enter date mm/dd/yy]

7 When the page is viewed in a browser the text in step 6 is displayed in the text box

Enter date mm/dd/yy

8 If text is entered by the user in an incorrect format the text box turns red and the text in step 5 is displayed

23/45/08   Invalid format.

9 If text is entered in the correct format the text box turns green and the user can proceed

01/01/08

Spry effects

Spry effects are visual devices that can be applied to images or text to create a variety of graphical effects.

To apply Spry effects:

 Select an image or a piece of text on a Dreamweaver page

2 Access the Behaviors panel (Window, Behaviors from the menu bar)

3 Click here on the Behaviors panel

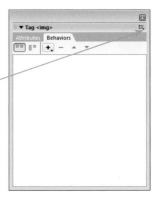

4 Click on Effects and select one of the available effects

5 Enter the properties for the selected effect and click OK

6 When the page is viewed in a browser, the item to which the Spry effect has been applied is displayed in its initial state (i.e. without the effect)

Beware

Use Spry effects sparingly as it can become irritating on a web page if there are a lot of items to which effects have been applied.

139

7 Once the action to trigger the effect is applied, the effect takes place (in this example the image is faded to the amount specified in step 5)

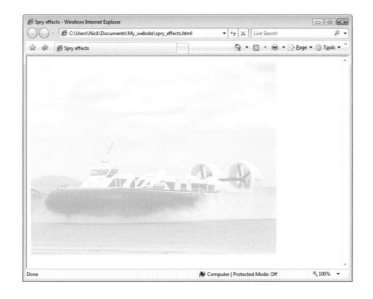

Spry data

Spry data is more complicated than Spry widgets or effects as it is used to manipulate data that has been created as a data set in an XML file. If you have created an XML data set, the Spry data functions can be used to allow users to manipulate the data once the web page has been published. For example, users could select an item in a table and this could be updated automatically, depending on the data in the XML data-set file.

To apply Spry data:

1 Click here on the Spry menu to select a data set

2 Click here to browse to the data set and click OK

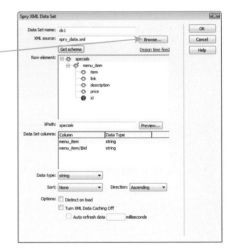

3 Select a Spry data item from the Spry menu (in this example it is a Spry Table)

4 Select the properties for the table and click OK to create the Spry Table

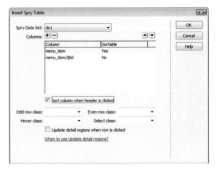

10 Assets

The process of creating websites can involve using the same basic designs and elements several times over. This chapter explains how Dreamweaver allows the web designer to repeat commonly used items across a website, through the use of elements in the Assets panel.

Managing assets

The Assets panel is an area that keeps track of many of the elements that you use in creating your websites. These include:

- Images
- Colors
- Hyperlinks
- Multimedia content such as Flash and Shockwave
- Video
- Scripts
- Templates
- Library items

You do not have to add items to the Assets panel (except for templates and Library items) since all of the relevant content is automatically added to the Assets panel when it is inserted into the Dreamweaver page. There are two ways to manage Assets: either on a site-wide basis, or as Favorites, which are usually items that you want to use on several pages. To view the site assets:

142

1 Select Window, Assets from the menu bar to access the Assets panel

2 Select the Site button and click on the Refresh button to view the assets for the current site

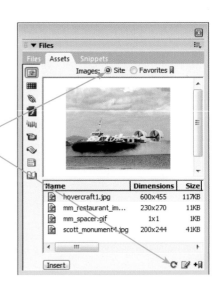

Creating Favorites

Assets that are going to be used regularly, such as an image that will appear on all the pages of a site, or a hyperlink back to the home page, can be added to the Favorites list for quick access. To do this:

Select an asset in the Site list and click here to add it to the Favorites

or

Select an item in Design view and right-click (Windows) or Ctrl+click (Mac) and select the relevant Add To command

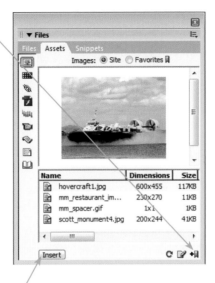

Applying assets

Assets are applied slightly differently depending on the item:

For images, Flash, Shockwave, video and scripts, select the item and then click on Insert to place it on the page

For colors and links, select the relevant item in Design view; then select the asset and click on Apply to have it take effect on the page

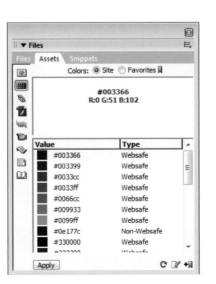

Using templates

Template files have been a common feature in word-processing and desktop-publishing programs for several years now. These are files that contain standard elements that recur in certain types of documents. The template can be used to store the recurring items, and new content can also be added once a document is opened using the template as a foundation. This is an excellent device for producing a consistent design for items such as newsletters and brochures, and it is also a time-saving device because the basic design only has to be created once.

Recognizing the value of templates for web designers, Dreamweaver has powerful facilities for creating and using templates. This means that designers can quickly create a consistent theme for a website, while still retaining the freedom to add new content to pages.

Templates in Dreamweaver can be created from scratch, or existing files can be converted into templates. New files can then be created, based on an existing template. It is also possible to edit the content of template files.

When templates are created you can specify which areas are constant, e.g. a company logo, and which are editable. This gives you a good degree of control over the pages that are created from your templates.

Some areas in a document created from a template remain static and cannot be edited, while others are fully editable. Editable regions are denoted by a green tag, with the name of the region.

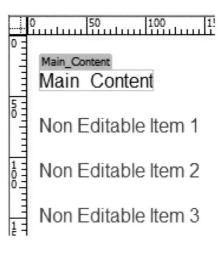

Don't forget

When a new document is opened from a template the document is based on the template, rather than being the template file itself. When it is first opened, the document will display the same content as the template file, but new items can then be added to the new document.

Don't forget

The colors for the tags in templates can be changed by selecting Edit, Preferences from the menu bar and then selecting Highlighting and a color for each of the regions within the template file.

144

Creating templates

Templates can be created from scratch or existing files can be converted into templates.

Creating a new template

1 Select File, New from the menu bar

2 Select Blank Template and a template type. Click OK

Don't forget

A template is identified in the document window with the word "Template" before its name in the address bar at the top of the Dreamweaver window.

3 Enter content for the template

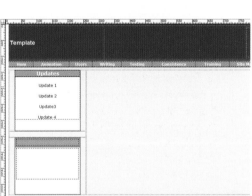

4 Click here and select Editable Region. This is the area to which content can be added in any pages created from the template

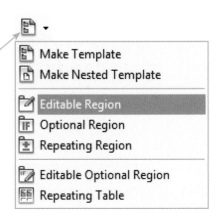

Don't forget

Dreamweaver templates are created with a .dwt extension rather than a .htm one.

...cont'd

5 Enter a name for the editable region and click OK

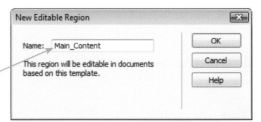

6 The Editable Region is inserted into the template and indicated by this tag

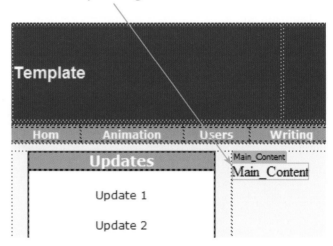

7 Select File, Save As Template from the menu bar. Select a site for the template and give it a name

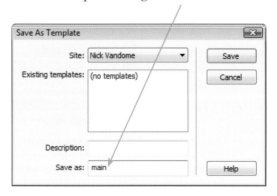

8 Click Save

Creating a template from an existing document

1 Open the document you want to use as a template

2 Click on the Editable Region button on the Common tab on the Insert bar

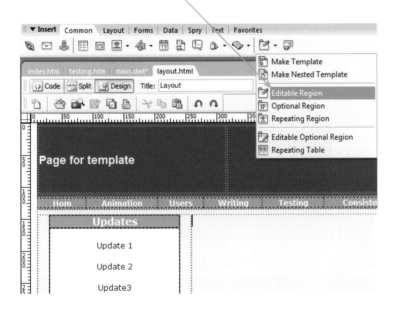

3 Since editable regions can only be inserted into templates, a message will appear saying that the file will be converted into a template file. Click OK

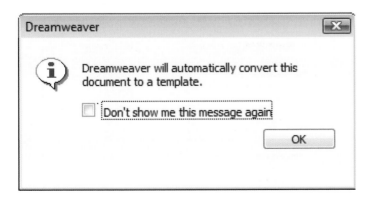

...cont'd

4 Enter a name for the new editable region

5 Click OK

6 The document is now an unsaved HTML file with the required editable region inserted

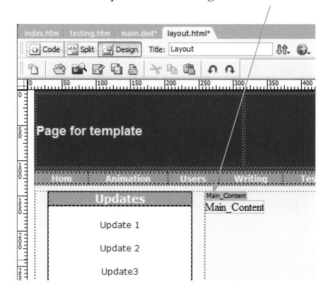

7 When the file is saved, it is done so as a template, in the same way as in steps 7 and 8 on page 146

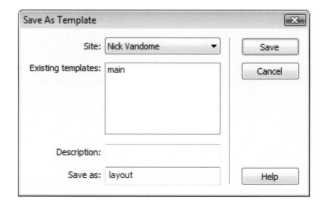

Creating template pages

Once templates have been created, it is then possible to produce new web pages in Dreamweaver, based on these templates. To do this:

1 Select File, New from the menu bar and click on Page from Template

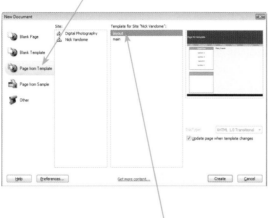

Don't forget

When templates are created, they are specific to the site in which they were produced. To use a template in another site, open it, select Save As Template from the Menu bar and then, in the Save As Template dialog box, select the site in which you want the template to be available.

2 Select a template that has already been created and click on Create

3 A new HTML document is opened, based on the selected template:

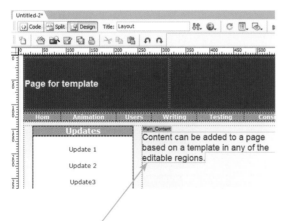

Don't forget

In a document based on a template, the outer border identifies the template on which the document is based and also the fact that everything within it is locked, unless it has been specified as an editable region.

4 The editable regions are displayed on the page and this is where content can be added

Editing templates

If you want to change the content of a particular template, this can be done by editing it. This changes the content for all of the documents that have been based on this template. So if you have ten documents based on a single template, the size of the headings in each one could be altered by editing the heading formatting in the template file. To edit a template:

1 Access the Assets panel by selecting Window, Assets from the menu bar

2 Click here to access the templates

3 Double-click on a template to open it

4 Edit the content of the template and select File, Save from the menu bar

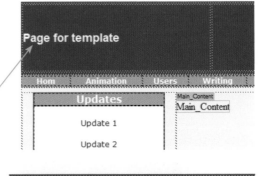

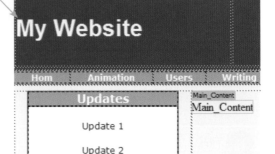

5 A dialog box will appear asking if you want to update all the documents based on this template. If you do, select Update

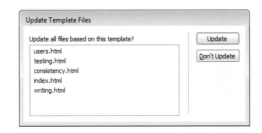

6 The Update Pages dialog box indicates when the update has been completed. Click Close once this has been done

7 The changes are made to all of the affected pages

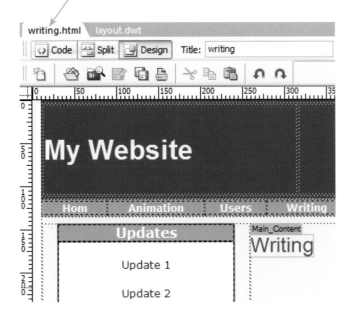

Repeating editable tables

In some cases it can be useful to create editable regions that can be repeated several times by the person creating documents based on the template. For instance, they may want to include table rows but are unsure how many they will want. If the row is created as a repeating editable region, they can add extra rows as they are needed. This also means that the basic structure of the template remains untouched, even though elements can be added to it. To create a repeating editable table:

1 Create a standard template and select an element within it

2 From the Common tab on the Insert panel, click here and select Repeating Table

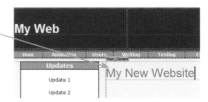

3 Enter details for the table and click OK

4 For pages created from the template the repeating table can be manipulated

using these buttons. Click on the plus sign to add a repeating region in the table and the minus sign to remove one. Use the up and down arrows to change the order of regions in the table

About the Library

During the design process of a website there will probably be some elements that you will want to reuse on different pages within the site. These could be static elements that appear on several pages, such as a company logo, or items where one part is updated regularly, such as a "latest news" section. Instead of having to create or insert these elements from their source locations each time you want to use them, Dreamweaver has a facility for storing them and then dragging them onto a page whenever they are required. The location in which they are stored is known as the Library. Each site can have its own individual Library, with items that are used throughout that site.

When an item is placed in the Library it creates a Library item file that links to the source location in which that item is stored. So if the item is an image, there will be a link to its location on the hard drive. This means that the image can be reused numerous times without increasing the file size of the page. Rather than placing a copy of the item on a page each time it is taken from the Library, Dreamweaver creates a reference (or instance) back to the source location of the item. As long as the item is not moved from its source location the Library version can be reused as many times as you like. Also, Library items can be updated, if required, and any changes made to them will be reflected in all of the instances of them in the site. To access the Library:

Hot tip

Before Library items can be created, the page from which they are being created has to be saved and placed within an existing site structure.

153

Click here on the Assets panel

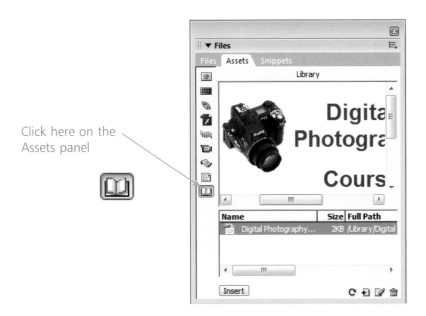

Creating Library items

Items can be added to the Library from any open Dreamweaver document. These will then be available in the Library to all other pages within that site. To add items to the Library:

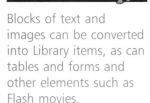
1 Open a file in Design view and make sure the Library panel is visible, as shown on the previous page

2 Select the item that you want to include in the Library

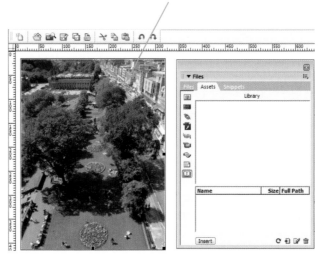

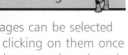
3 Drag and drop the item into either panel of the Library

4 Type a name for the Library item

Adding Library items

Once items have been created in the Library, they can then be reused on any page within the site structure. To do this:

1 Select an item in the Library

2 Drag and drop the selected Library item onto the Design-view page

or

Click on the Insert button on the Library panel

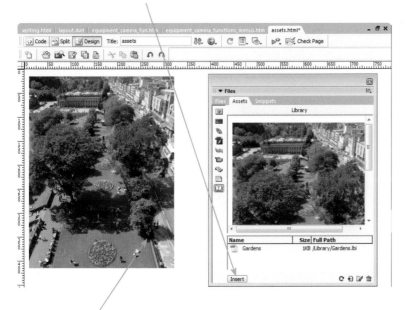

3 An instance of the Library item is placed on the page. This is locked, i.e. it cannot be edited within the document itself

Don't forget

Library items are created as individual files with a .lib extension.

Don't forget

Once a Library item has been added to a document, it will remain there even if it is subsequently deleted from the Library.

155

Don't forget

To change the color used to highlight Library items when they are placed in a document, select Edit, Preferences from the menu bar, select Highlighting as the category and select a color from the box next to Library Items.

Editing Library items

Library items are very versatile in that it is possible to edit them in the Library itself, in which case the changes apply to all of the instances of these items throughout the site, or individual Library items in a document can be made editable so that they can then be edited independently.

Editing items in the Library

If you open and edit an item in the Library itself, these changes can be applied to all occurrences of that item throughout a whole site. To do this:

Don't forget

When a Library item is opened, it is done so in a separate window, with the words "Library Item" in the title.

Don't forget

A Library item can also be edited by clicking on the arrow at the top of the Assets panel and selecting Edit.

1 Open an item in the Library by double-clicking the name or by selecting it and clicking the Edit button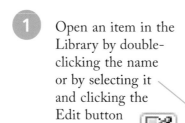

2 In the Library Item window, make editing changes to the item. Select File, Save from the menu bar to apply the changes

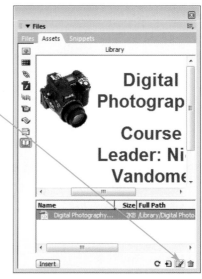

3 The Update Library Items dialog box will appear. If you want to update this item in all of the files in which it occurs, click Update

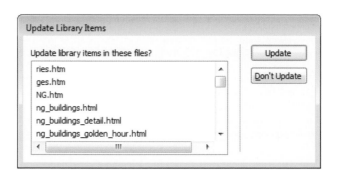

Editing Library items in a document

After a Library item has been placed in a document it is still possible to perform certain editing tasks on it:

1 Select a Library item on a document page by clicking on it once. It will not be possible to edit this directly

2 The Library Properties box will be displayed

Click "Detach from original" to detach the item in the document from the source Library item. This means that it can be edited in the document window, but it will not have any changes applied to it if the source Library item is edited

Click Open to open the item in the Library window. The content can then be edited

Click Recreate to recreate a Library item, if the original has been deleted from the Library palette

Editable navigation bars

A navigation bar is a set of buttons that can help the user navigate between the most commonly used areas or pages of a website. They can appear at the top or the side of all pages throughout a site. This has the advantage of creating a uniform style and it makes the user feel comfortable within the site. For information about creating navigation bars, see Chapter 7, page 118. One of the possible drawbacks with navigation bars is that if you have them throughout your site and then decide to update a link within them, it can be a laborious task. This can be greatly simplified by creating the navigation bar as a Library item:

Hot tip

If you have a site that contains a navigation bar on several hundred pages you will soon come to appreciate the importance of creating it as a Library item so that it can be updated site-wide in a single operation.

Beware

After updating a Library item, make sure that all of the relevant files are uploaded to the remote site, i.e. the one that is hosting the website.

 Create a navigation bar and convert it into a Library item by dragging it into one of the Library panels

 Click here to edit the navigation bar

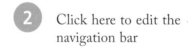 Apply the editing and select File, Save from the menu bar

You will be prompted as to whether you want to update all of the pages that contain this Library item. Click Update

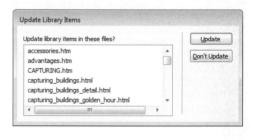

11 Advanced features

This chapter looks at some of the more advanced features in Dreamweaver, such as forms, layers, Flash content, scripts and mobile devices and shows how they can be used to create high-quality, professional sites.

Forms

An HTML form is a set of objects that the user can interact with to send various pieces of information to the server hosting the web page, or directly to the author of the page, which require a piece of computer programming called a script. This can collate the information from the form, analyze it and send it to a specified location. This can be done with a variety of scripting languages, such as Perl or Javascript. The script can either be placed within the form itself (client-side) or on the server that will be processing the information (server-side). If it is a server-side application, this is usually handled with a Common Gateway Interface script.

A form can be made up of several different elements, all of which are contained in an overall form container. Attributes and properties can then be assigned to each element within the form structure. To create a form and set its properties:

1 Click the Forms tab on the Insert panel

2 Click the Form button to add the form container

The properties for a form are entered in the Form Properties Inspector and they are:

- Form Name. This is a unique identifier for the form

- Action. If the form is being processed by a server-side script, enter the URL of the script here

- Method. This is the way information is sent to the server. The options are Get, Post and Default

- Enctype. The type of encryption used if the form needs to be secure, e.g. if it deals with financial transactions

Form elements

There are a variety of elements that can be added to forms and these are accessed from the Forms tab on the Insert panel. The available options are:

- Text Field. This can be used to enter single lines of data, multiple lines of data or passwords

- Hidden Field. This can be inserted into a form to capture information about the user, or the form itself

- Textarea. Similar to a text field except that it contains scroll bars so that unlimited text can be entered

- Checkbox. This can be used with a list of options that the user has to select as required. In a list of check boxes, numerous items can be selected: it is not an either–or option

- Radio Button. These are similar to check boxes, except that they only allow for a single option to be selected

- Radio Group. This allows for groups of radio buttons to be inserted, with each group containing a different option

- List/Menu. Creates a drop-down list or menu

- Jump Menu. Creates a drop-down menu with items that contain a hyperlink to another page or object

- Image Field. This can be used to insert an image into a form, generally for design purposes

- File Field. This allows the user to select a file from their hard drive and enter it into the form

- Button. This can be used to insert Submit or Reset buttons

- Label. This is an optional button that can be used to give textual labels to form elements

- Fieldset. This is a container for a group of related form elements

- Spry elements. These are Spry elements that can be used within a form. For more information on Spry elements see Chapter 9

Hot tip

A form has a non-printing border that can be used to help format items within the form. If this is not visible when the form is inserted, select View, Visual Aids, Invisible Elements from the menu bar.

Hot tip

Forms take on the background color of the page on which they are created. However, text and images can be formatted independently within a form. Tables can also be inserted within a form and the form elements placed inside them for formatting purposes.

Frames

Traditionally frames have had an uneasy relationship with the Web, primarily for two reasons:

- They can cause problems for older browsers, such as those earlier than Internet Explorer 3 and Netscape Navigator 3, and they can also cause problems for search engines

- They are one of the harder concepts for web designers to master, particularly those new to this medium

The basic concept of frames is that the content of two or more pages is displayed on screen at the same time. Each page is known as a frame and numerous frames can be displayed at the same time. Each frame acts independently of the others that are being displayed; so it is possible to scroll through the contents of one frame, while all of the others remain static. The final part of the frames equation is the frameset. This is the document that contains all of the frames that are being viewed. So if there are two frames on a page, this involves three documents: the two frame pages and the frameset. The frameset is a separate HTML document that has no visible content of its own. Instead it contains a command for the browser to display the frames that it specifies. It can also contain other details of how to display the frames.

To create frames and framesets:

Beware

If possible, try and avoid using frames for creating websites. Instead, use templates to create a consistent look for sites.

1 Select File, New from the menu bar

2 Select Page from Sample and click on Framesets. Select the required design. Click Create

3 The selected style opens in the document window

4 The Properties Inspector displays the currently selected frame

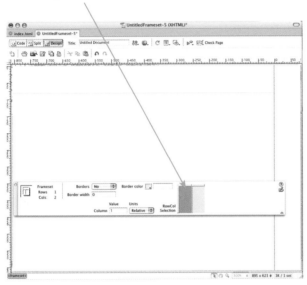

Hot tip

If some content is not visible in a frame, the frame's borders can be resized by dragging them (see next page).

5 Add content by clicking in each frame and adding content in the same way as for any other file

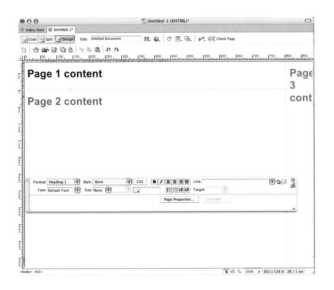

...cont'd

Don't forget

Each frame can be given a unique name in the Properties Inspector. This can be useful when adding hyperlinks between frames.

Beware

Hyperlinks can be added to frames in the same way as to other HTML files. However, to make sure they open up in the correct location, use the Target box in the Properties Inspector. This will let you select a specific location for where the linked file opens. Some practice is required when working with links in frames.

6 Drag the frame borders to change their sizes

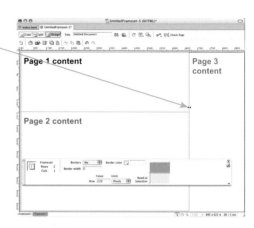

7 Once content has been added to each frame, select File, Save All from the menu bar

8 Give a name for the frameset and click Save

9 Give each individual frame a name and click Save. You will be prompted to save each frame until all of the elements of the frameset have been saved

Layers

Layers are independent blocks of content that can be added to web pages. They can be moved around pages and they are treated as div tags in the code. Layers can be a very flexible way of adding and positioning certain elements of content. To add layers:

1 Select the Layout tab on the Insert panel and click here

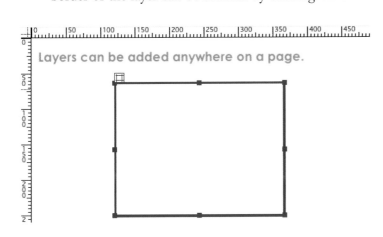

2 Draw a layer by dragging in the document window. The border of the layer can be selected by clicking on it once

Layers can be added anywhere on a page.

3 Click within the layer and add content in the normal way. All content types can be added within a layer

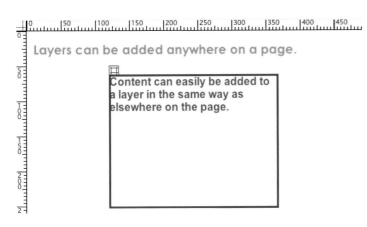

Layers can be added anywhere on a page.

Content can easily be added to a layer in the same way as elsewhere on the page.

165

Don't forget

In Dreamweaver CS3, layers are known as AP Elements and details of them can be viewed in the AP Elements panel.

Beware

Layers do not always display as expected in all browsers, particularly older ones. Always check layers in a variety of browsers before they are published.

Don't forget

Layers can be used to overlap different items of content on a page.

...cont'd

4 The code for the layer is automatically created within a div tag. This means that it can be positioned accurately on the page

```
<body>
<div id="apDiv1">
  <h2>Content can easily be added to a layer in the same way <br />
as elsewhere on the page.</h2>
</div>
```

5 Select Window, CSS Styles from the menu bar. The Layer is automatically created as a new CSS rule and can be edited accordingly

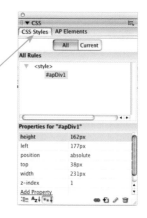

Hot tip

The "layer z-index" in the Properties Inspector determines the stacking order of layers if they are placed on top of each other. The higher the number, the further up in the stacking order a layer is. For instance, a layer with a z-index of 2 would appear above a layer with a z-index of 1.

6 Click here and drag to move the layer to a new location (this change will be reflected within the CSS Styles panel)

Layers can be added anywhere on a page.

Content can easily be added to a layer in the same way as elsewhere on the page.

7 Select a layer and its properties are displayed in the Properties Inspector

Flash buttons and text

Flash is an animation program that has become the industry standard for producing animated effects on the Web. As with Dreamweaver, it is also produced by Adobe, and in Dreamweaver CS3 some of the power of Flash has been harnessed through the use of animated buttons and text. This allows web designers in Dreamweaver to create buttons and text that change appearance when the user moves the cursor over them. To create Flash buttons or text (the process is almost exactly the same for both; this example is for a button):

Hot tip

Entire Flash movies can also be imported into Dreamweaver documents. To do this, create a movie in Flash, then select the Insert Flash button on the Common tab on the Insert panel and select the required file.

1 Select Flash Button (or Flash Text) on the Common tab on the Insert panel

2 Select a pre-designed style for the button

3 Add the text you want to appear on the button

4 Enter a hyperlink for the button

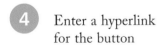

5 Click OK

6 Select the button and click Play in the Properties Inspector to view the effect when the cursor is passed over it

Beware

If you are using Flash buttons or text, the users will have to have the Flash Player installed on their computer in order to view your Flash effects. This can be downloaded from the Adobe website at www.adobe.com.

167

Behaviors

Behaviors in Dreamweaver are pre-programmed events that are triggered by the user performing a certain action on the page. For instance, the action of rolling the cursor over an image could trigger the event of a sound being played. Behaviors are created by Javascript programming but Dreamweaver contains several pre-written behaviors that can be inserted into a page using the Behaviors Inspector.

Creating a behavior consists of two parts, defining the action that is going to be performed and stating the event that will be triggered by the action. There are several events that can be selected and more can be downloaded from the Web. When an event is selected the action to trigger it is automatically included. To create a behavior:

Hot tip

If you want to attach a behavior to a whole page, create it without selecting anything within the document. This behavior is usually triggered when the file is opened, on the Web, and is identified by the onLoad event.

168

1 Select an item to which you want to attach a behavior, such as an image

Don't forget

The script for behaviors is inserted into the head portion of the HTML source code. If you know Javascript you can write your own scripts and include them as behaviors.

2 Click the Behaviors tab from within the Tag Inspector

3 Click here to access the Actions menu. Select the action that you want to use for the selected item

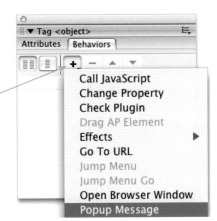

4 The action is entered and the default event (the one that will trigger the action) is inserted. Here it is onMouseOver, which means the action will be triggered when the cursor is rolled over the selected item

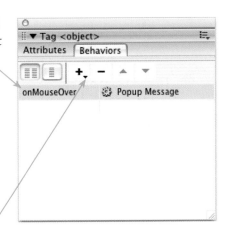

5 Click here to access alternative options for the default event, if any are available

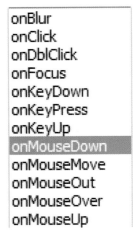

Don't forget

The events associated with selected images, text or hyperlinks include: onMouseOver, which is when the cursor is moved over the selected item; onMouseOut, which is when the cursor is moved off the selected item; and onClick, which is when the selected item is clicked.

169

Javascript

In Dreamweaver, some effects, such as rollover buttons, are created using a programming language called Javascript. This is a popular language for use on the Web and it can be inserted into web pages for a variety of purposes, such as producing scrolling text or dates that update themselves automatically. If you are proficient in writing Javascript, it is possible to write and insert this code yourself. (It is also possible to include other scripting languages such as VBScript.) To insert Javascript into a Dreamweaver page:

Don't forget

Scripts can be entered while you are working in Design view or Code view, or a combination of both.

1 Click the Script button on the HTML tab on the Insert panel

2 Click Script to select the type of script to write

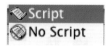

3 In the Content box, enter your script

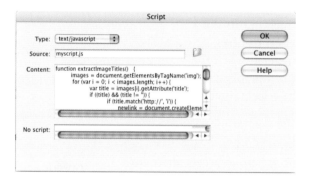

Hot tip

To learn Javascript, look at "Javascript in Easy Steps" in this series.

4 Click OK to insert the script into a file

5 On the toolbar, click here to validate your script

Don't forget

For an in-depth look at Javascript and Dreamweaver, select Help, Dreamweaver Help from the menu bar and select Javascript from the index or enter it into the search box.

Dynamic web pages

Among the most important developments with web pages in recent years are dynamic web pages. These are websites and pages that interact with databases: the pages displayed change depending on the database or the information requested by the users. Dynamic web pages can be created with server technologies, including programming languages such as ColdFusion, Javascript and Active Server Pages (ASP). Dreamweaver CS3 provides comprehensive support for these technologies to enable developers to work more easily with dynamic pages.

In order to create dynamic web pages you will require a good understanding of the relevant server technology. However, Dreamweaver CS3 makes it as painless as possible to produce the initial structure. To do this for dynamic pages:

1 Select File, New from the menu bar

2 Select Blank Page and one of the dynamic page options, or

3 Select Other and one of these options

4 For the selected item, click on the Data tab on the Insert toolbar. The available item can be used to add content for the selected dynamic-page type

Don't forget

The server technologies supported by Dreamweaver CS3 are ColdFusion, ASP, ASP.NET, JSP, and PHP. This means that you can create dynamic content with these languages and Dreamweaver will be able to display the results, as long as you have a web server (see the tip below).

Don't forget

In order to create and test dynamic web pages you will need to have a web server installed on your computer. This is a program that interprets the dynamic content and serves the results to a browser. Different server technologies use different web servers but some of them are interchangeable. Three types of web server are the Personal Web Server, the Internet Information Server (both from Microsoft) and Apache. The web server is used as the Testing Server in Dreamweaver.

XML

Another major recent development in web-page design is the emergence of XML (Extensible Markup Language). Although this is similar in some ways to HTML, it enables you to create your own custom tags and produce pages that can interact effectively with databases and convert the information so that it can be viewed in an HTML document. XML is usually used in conjunction with HTML to produce documents known as XHTML. XML is a stricter language than HTML and if it is not written accurately it will not work. Like dynamic web pages, this is a fairly complex subject, but Dreamweaver provides the means to get started:

Beware

XML is a lot more complicated to use than HTML. For a comprehensive look at this subject, see the websites www.xml.com and www.w3.org/xml.

Hot tip

For more detail about XML, take a look at "XML in Easy Steps".

Don't forget

In XML most elements have opening and closing tags, as with HTML. However, if an element does not have a closing tag (usually an element that does not have any textual output) it has to be closed with the forward-slash symbol and a closing bracket: "/>". So a tag for an image could look like this:

<image="nick1.jpg"/>

1 Select File, New from the menu bar. Select XML under Blank Page and click Create. This creates the start of an XML page

2 Create the XML content. None of the graphical authoring tools are available in this environment

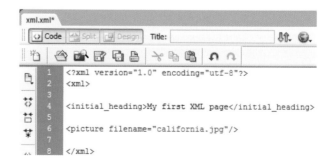

Designing for mobile devices

As web users become more and more sophisticated they are looking to have their content delivered in a variety of different ways, particularly to mobile devices such as cellphones and personal digital assistants (PDAs). This presents a considerable challenge for designers as they have to be aware that users may be looking at their content on devices that have considerably smaller screens than standard computers. It is therefore useful to be able to see how content designed in Dreamweaver will appear on mobile devices. This can be done with a feature known as Device Central. To use this:

Don't forget

Files have to be saved before they can be previewed in the Device Central environment.

1 Open or create a Dreamweaver file. Click here on the Document toolbar and select Preview in Device Central

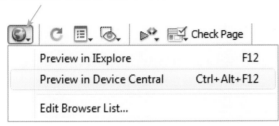

2 The content is displayed on a sample device

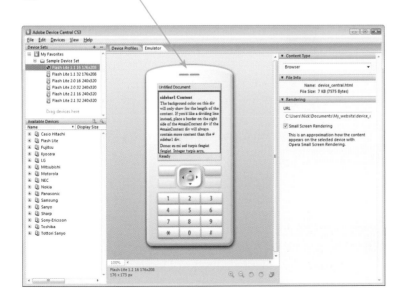

173

...cont'd

3 Click here to select specific devices on which to preview the content

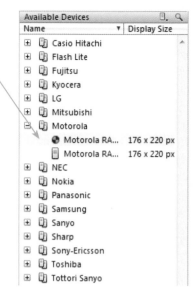

4 Click on the Device Profiles tab to view the properties of specific devices, as selected in step 3

5 Depending on how the previewed content appears, it can, if necessary, then be edited in Dreamweaver to make it display more effectively on specific mobile devices

12 Publishing

This chapter shows how to publish a site on the Internet or on an internal network. It also explains how to work with files once a site has been published and it is live.

Site management

The final step before publishing a site is to check it thoroughly to make sure that everything is working properly. This involves making sure all of the links work and that everything looks the way it should. One way to do this is to preview the site in a browser and go through all of the pages. This can be done by pressing F12 or selecting File, Preview in Browser. Another option is to check all of the hyperlinks in the site window. This will generate a list of all of the broken links in your site and you can then take remedial action. To check the accuracy of the links in your entire site:

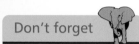

1 In the Files panel, select the site that you want to check by clicking here

2 Click here and select Site, Check Links Sitewide from the Site-panel menu bar

3 If there are any broken links in your site they will be listed in the Link Checker panel

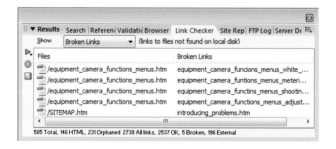

4 To mend a broken link, click on its URL and type in the correct address, or open the relevant file in the document window, select the broken link and add a new link

Checking files in and out

If you are working on a corporate website or an intranet it is likely that you will not be the only person working on the files that are in the site structure. If this is the case, it is important to know who is working on a certain file at a particular time. This avoids any duplication of work and ensures that the correct version of a file is uploaded to the live site.

Dreamweaver uses a system to ensure that only one person can be working on a file at a time, no matter how many other people there are in the team of web designers. This is known as checking files in and out. For this to work properly it has to be activated, and then individuals can check files in and out as required.

Enabling checking in and out

① Select Site, Manage Sites from the menu bar

② In the Manage Sites dialog box select the required site and click Edit

③ In the Site Definition dialog box, select the Remote Info category and check the "Enable file check in and check out" box. Click OK

Beware

If file checking in and out is not used, then it is possible for more than one person to be working on a file at a time, if it is in a shared environment. Unless you are the sole author of a website, it is recommended that file checking in and out is turned on.

177

Hot tip

When the "Enable file check in and check out" box is checked, this activates another option, for adding the name that you want to use as identification when you are checking files in and out. Make sure it is something that the rest of the design team will recognize easily.

Using the site map

The site map provides a graphical representation of a site and it can be used to perform various management tasks before the site is published.

Checking the structure

Use the site map to check the overall structure of a site. This can also be used to display broken links within a site:

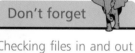

Don't forget

To open a page directly from the site window, double-click on it. It will then be opened in Design view and it can be edited there.

1 In the Files panel, click here to expand the panel

2 Click here to access the site map

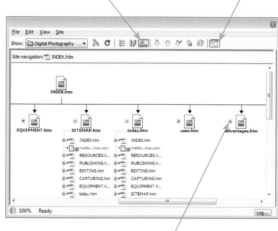

3 The top two levels of the site are displayed. Click on a plus sign to see the linked files below the second level

Within the site map the following symbols and notation are used:

- Red text, or a broken-chain link icon, represents a broken hyperlink on the site

- Blue text with a globe icon indicates a link to a file outside the current site structure or an item such as an email link

- Green and red ticks represent files that are checked in or out

- A padlock icon represents files that are read-only (Windows) or locked (Mac)

Don't forget

Checking files in and out are functions that are used when more than one person is working on the same website. They let everyone know who is working on a specific file.

Formatting the site map

The appearance of the site map can be customized to suit your own preferences:

1 Select Site, Manage Sites from the menu bar

2 Select the required site and click Edit

3 In the Site Definition dialog box, click on the Site Map Layout category

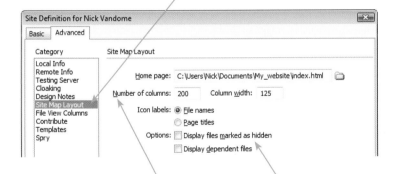

4 Enter values for the way the columns of information are displayed

5 Under "Icon labels", set whether files are displayed by page title or file name

6 Specify whether hidden or dependent files are displayed

Hot tip

You can add new files to a site from within the site map and link them directly to existing files. To do this, click once on a file in the site map. Select Site, Link to New File (Windows) or Site, Site Map View, Link to New File (Mac) from the Files-panel menu bar. In the Link to New File dialog box enter a filename for the new file, a page title and the text that will act as a link in the current file to the new one. Select OK and the new file will be inserted in the site map. Double-click on the initially selected file to open it and view the link to the new file.

Uploading a site

Once you have checked your site structure and made sure that there are no broken links on a site, it is time to upload it onto the server that is going to be hosting the site. If you are working on an internal intranet, then the server will probably be part of your local network and the IT systems administrator will be able to advise you about the procedure for uploading a website. If your site is being hosted on the Internet by your Internet service provider (ISP), you will have to obtain from them the relevant settings needed when a website is being uploaded.

The process of uploading, or publishing, a website in Dreamweaver consists of creating an exact copy on the remote server of all of the items within your local site structure. This includes all of the HTML files, images and other elements that have been included in your site. The same site structure is also retained, so that all of the links in your site will match their target destinations and so work properly.

To upload a site

1 Select Site, Manage Sites from the menu bar

2 In the Manage Sites dialog box, select a site and select Edit

Hot tip

A lot of ISPs have online advice about uploading your own website and the settings that will be required. Try looking under their "Help" or "Technical Support" links. If possible, try to avoid telephoning, since a lot of ISPs charge premium rates for calls to their helplines. Emailing could be a useful compromise if you do not want to telephone.

Don't forget

When you upload a site to an FTP server, the ISP hosting the site will assign it a web address (URL). This will probably be based on your own username.

3 In the Advanced panel of the Site Definition dialog box, select the Remote Info category

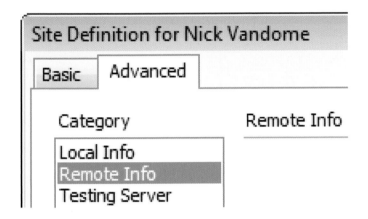

Don't forget

You will have to get the exact FTP settings from the ISP that is going to be hosting your site. In general terms the details that are needed are:

•FTP host. This is the name for identifying the host computer system on the Internet. It is not the same as a web address (URL) or an email address

•Host directory. This is the location on the host's server where your site will be stored

•Login. This is the login name you will use to access your site's files

•Password. This is the password that you will use to access your site's files

4 Click on Access and select FTP if the site is going to be published on the Web, or Local/Network if it is going to be published on an internal network

Remote Info

Access: FTP

5 In the Remote Info section of the Site Definition dialog box enter details for the FTP host, the host directory, the login and the password. (Not all ISPs require host-directory data, as these are assigned automatically.) When this has been done, click OK (currently hidden) in the dialog box

...cont'd

Beware

The Connect button is grayed out, i.e. not available, if the FTP settings have not been entered. However, when it becomes available this is no guarantee that the FTP settings have been entered correctly.

Beware

If you have a lot of images in your site structure, or a few large ones, then your site will take longer to upload to the FTP server than if they were not there. This will give you some idea of how long users will have to wait for certain items to download.

Don't forget

If you experience problems when you try and upload a site with FTP, select View, Site FTP Log from the Site-panel menu bar. This may give you some indication of the problem.

6   In the Manage Sites dialog box, click Done

7   In the Files panel, click the Connect button. This will connect you to your ISP or local network

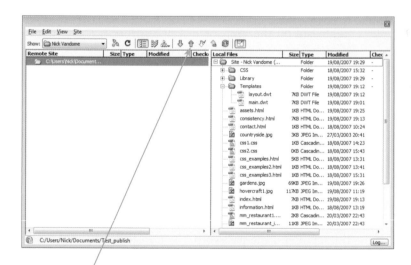

8   Select the root folder and click the Put button. If the site has been uploaded successfully, the remote folder should be visible in the Remote Site panel and contain a mirror image of the local site

Getting and putting files

If you want to edit a file on your site you can do so either by opening it in the document window and then uploading it to the remote site once the changes have been made, or by opening it from the remote site itself and then making the changes. This involves using the Put and Get commands: Put transfers files from the local folder to the remote server and Get does the reverse.

Putting files

If a file has been edited and updated, the Put command can be used to place it on the remote server:

1 In the Files panel, select the file in the local folder by clicking on it once

2 Click the Put button. Dreamweaver will connect to the remote network and place the file in the remote folder

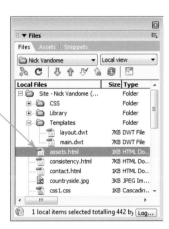

Getting files

1 In the Files panel click here and select the Remote View

2 Select a file or a folder and click the Get button to get the selected item from the remote site

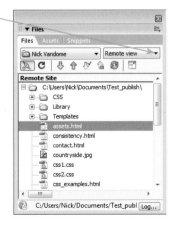

Cloaking

Cloaking is a publishing device that can be used to prevent certain folders or file types being published. This can be useful if you are working on some draft pages or if you want to exclude certain large file types from being published every time you update a site. To use cloaking:

If you want to cloak specific files you have to do this by cloaking the file type in the Site Definition dialog box. This could cause problems if, for instance, you wanted to cloak an HTML file, as all of the other HTML files in the site would also be cloaked. If you do want to cloak specific files, place them in a new folder and apply cloaking to the folder.

Hot tip

If you want to specify more than one file type to be cloaked, separate the different types with a single space in the "Cloak files ending with" box. Do not use a comma or a semicolon.

Beware

Cloaked items are excluded from site-management tasks such as synchronizing and updating templates and Library items. However, these functions can still be performed by selecting the folder or file individually, as this overrides any cloaking commands.

184

1 Select Site, Manage Sites from the menu bar

2 In the Manage Sites dialog box select a site and click Edit

3 Select the Advanced tab and the Cloaking category

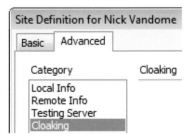

4 Check the "Enable cloaking" box

Options: ☑ Enable cloaking

Cloaking lets you exclude specified folders and files from all site operations.

5 Check the "Cloak files ending with" box and enter any required file types

☑ Cloak files ending with:

.png .fla

6 Click OK at the bottom of the dialog box

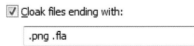

Applying cloaking

Cloaking can be applied to folders but not individual files (these have to be cloaked by applying a file type to be cloaked in the Site Definition dialog box, as shown on the previous page). To cloak folders:

1 Select a folder in the Files panel

2 Click here to access the Files-panel menu

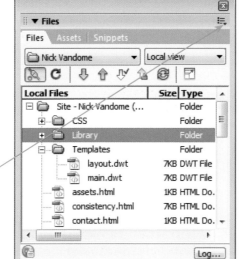

3 Select Site, Cloaking, Cloak from the menu to cloak the selected folder

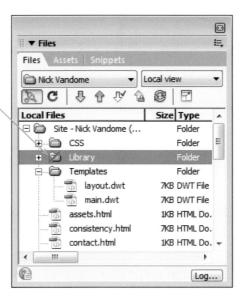

Beware

If you are developing draft sites, make sure they are cloaked when you are publishing other files and folders.

Don't forget

Once a folder or file type has been cloaked a red line is placed through it in the Site panel.

185

Don't forget

Cloaked items can be uncloaked by selecting them in the Site panel and selecting Cloaking, Uncloak from the Site-panel menu.

Synchronizing files

When you are updating and editing files and checking them in and out, it is easy to lose track of whether the most recent version of a file is in the local folder or on the remote site. Dreamweaver offers a solution to this problem, in the form of file synchronization. This automatically updates both the local and the remote sites so that the most recent version of all the site files is placed in each location. To synchronize files between the local and remote sites:

Don't forget

If you only want to synchronize certain files, select them first in the local or the remote folder and then select Selected Local Files Only in the Synchronize menu of the Synchronize Files dialog box.

1 In the Files panel, select Site, Synchronize from the menu bar

2 In the Synchronize Files dialog box, select whether you want to synchronize the entire site or only the files in the local site

Don't forget

Once the synchronization options have been selected, Dreamweaver connects to the remote site to check the versions of the files there. Therefore, make sure your Internet connection is active when you want to perform any synchronization.

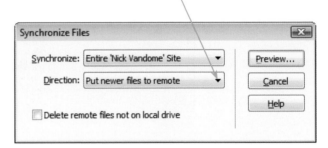

3 Click Preview to see the files that will be updated

Don't forget

If the latest versions of all files are in both the remote and the local site folders then a message will appear stating this and saying that nothing requires to be synchronized.

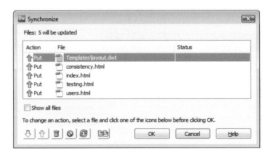

4 Click OK

Index

I

J

L

M

189

X

Z